LOTHIAN
AUSTRALIAN
garden
SERIES

Gardening with Australian Plants

Series Editor: **John Patrick**

Rodger Elliot

LOTHIAN PUBLISHING COMPANY PTY LTD
Melbourne • Sydney • Auckland

Acknowledgements

With any gardening book there are always people on which you call for help, advice or to request permission to take photographs of their gardens. Those who deserve special mention are John and Julie Bird, Beryl and Trevor Blake, Kath Deery, Kevin Hoffman, Diana and Brian Snape, A. Ross Lloyd and Paul Thompson — Thanks!

Once again Gwen, my best friend and wife has been of incalculable value as she has contributed indomitably in her roles as research assistant, editor and word processing activist. This book has greatly benefited from her input.

A Lothian Book
Lothian Publishing Company Pty Ltd
11 Munro Street, Port Melbourne,
Victoria 3207

Copyright © W. Rodger Elliot 1990
Copyright illustrations © Lothian Publishing
Company Pty Ltd 1990
First published 1990

National Library of Australia
Cataloguing-in-Publication data:

Elliot, W. R. (Winston Rodger), 1941–
    Gardening with Australian plants.

    Includes index.
    ISBN 0 85091 403 5.

    1. Wild flower gardening – Australia. I. Title.
    (Series: Lothian Australian garden guide
    series).

635.95194

Design Marius Foley/David Spratt
Line drawings Julia McLeish
Cover design David Constable
Typeset in Cheltenham and Rockwell
by Bookset Pty Ltd
Printed in Australia by Impact Printing

Foreword

The popularity of Australia's native flora is considerable. Nobody has done more to champion their cause and to instruct gardeners in their use than Rodger Elliot, who through his readable and easily comprehensible approach to the subject ensures more converts with each of his books.

The use of our native flora is now more sophisticated than ever. Colour and texture as a basis for selection is beginning to take on an importance while more and more gardeners are experimenting with coppicing, pollarding and clipping shrubs and trees to develop exciting and unusual effects in the garden. These approaches have been the basis for gardening with exotic plants for centuries and their application in our gardens to our flora is long overdue.

Rodger Elliot tackles many of these issues in this book, suited to beginner and enthusiast alike. It will earn him new admirers and should see the beginning of more gardeners using Australia's wonderful flora everywhere.

JOHN PATRICK
Series Editor

Contents

Introduction

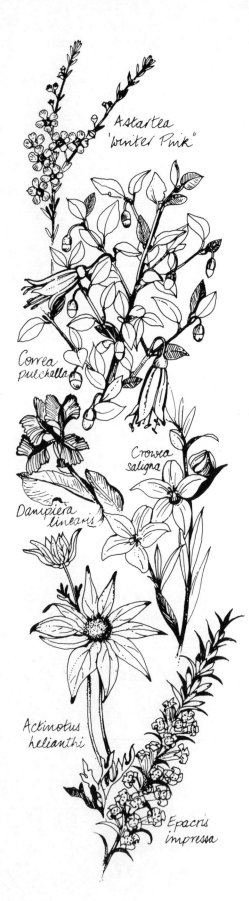

Astartea 'Winter Pink'

Correa pulchella

Crowea saligna

Dampiera linearis

Actinotus helianthi

Epacris impressa

If you have more than a passing interest in plants, then Australia is one of the most exciting places in the world. It has many unique and fascinating plants which help to make up one of the richest natural floras in the world. Australia is home to plants of all shapes and sizes. They can produce intriguing and exquisite flowers, some of which have beautiful perfumes. The foliage contrasts in colour, shape and fragrance are wonderful.

There are over 25,000 different flowering Australian plants, of which around 75 per cent occur naturally nowhere else in the world. They are unique to Australia or, to use the botanical term, endemic in Australia. The remaining 25 per cent or so are indigenous, and are also distributed beyond Australia.

For some reason Australian plants are often depicted as dull and uninteresting. This is a myth! We have only to consider the splendour of wattle in full bloom; the intricacies of minute trigger plants with their pseudo-mechanical triggers which brush the backs of visiting insects in order to spread pollen from one flower to another; the wealth of blue-flowering plants, with some dampieras providing a vivid carpet during spring and summer; bizarre and beautiful kangaroo paws in vibrant colours which flower through summer and entice nectar-seeking birds to bounce and sway on the slender stems as they extend their long and thin brush-tipped tongues deep into the floral tube for the sweet nectar. The birds may then move on to other summer-flowering plants for food, including melaleucas and beaufortias, shrubby relatives of Australia's magnificent eucalypts. Australia has a wonderful variety of native birds, with a fantastic range of songs and coloured plumages and for many Australians the fascination of observing native birds in their gardens is one of the main reasons for cultivating Australian plants. These plants and birds are an intrinsic part of our natural heritage which most Australians have come to treasure, and wish to preserve and conserve.

For millions of years the continent of Australia has been isolated from the rest of the world so its plants have developed features and characteristics which differ in many ways from plants of other countries. Of course, there are plants with strong links to other regions, from the time when Australia was still part of the great land mass before the continental drift. Some of the same Australian plant species also occur in tropical Asia, New Guinea, New Zealand and New Caledonia, while closely allied plants are found in South Africa and the west coast of South America.

The diversity of soils and climatic conditions in Australia is mind boggling. Australia is renowned as the driest continent (after Antarctica), with huge expanses of arid, sandy and stony deserts but, at the other end of the scale, outstanding tropical rainforests (now much depleted), which in some areas stop right on the ocean's edge. There are snow-covered alpine regions, tall mountains, sandplains, swamps, gorges and extensive river systems, some of which are ephemeral. These conditions have been instrumental in the development of an extremely wide range of plants which have adapted to survive, and in some cases thrive, in often inhospitable situations.

We are fortunate to have within Australia a wealth of wonderful, and in some cases peculiar, plants, many of which have unlimited potential for cultivation. Of course, some of these plants have stringent cultivation requirements, but others are extremely adaptable. One example is the native frangipani, *Hymenosporum flavum*, which is a rainforest plant, but you will find it growing successfully in almost all parts of Australia. Callistemons or bottlebrushes are another group which springs to mind as being amongst the most adaptable of Australian plants.

Recent years have seen a tremendous upsurge in interest in the cultivation of Australian plants, and with it, increased knowledge about the requirements of particular plants. There is now also a much greater emphasis on local or indigenous plants because a growing number of people realise that so much of our natural heritage has disappeared or is under threat from suburbanisation and agricultural development. By using indigenous plants the character of a local area can be enhanced.

Selections of horticulturally desirable species have been made and limited hybridisation programmes have resulted in some excellent new introductions to the horticultural scene. Many of the hybrids initially introduced into cultivation were the result of chance crosses occurring in gardens and, although some were exceptional, many lacked characteristics which were an improvement on those of the parents.

The potential of Australian plants is starting to be realised. There is an absolute boom in the number of species being grown for the cut-flower trade — both as fresh and dried flowers — and there is an active search for further information on species useful for food and medicinal purposes.

We are coming to know and appreciate more than ever the beauty of Australian plants and their value in cultivation. As gardening with Australian plants is virtually in its infancy, we have the exciting opportunity to be pioneers and share in discovering the delights which unfold as we cultivate small clump-forming species, groundcovers, small trees, majestic tall trees, delicate annuals, shrubs of varying sizes and climbers, vigorous or not so vigorous.

We are able to cultivate recently discovered species and there are still many awaiting discovery. What prospects!

By gardening with Australian plants you are able to pursue your personal tastes with almost limitless scope for individual creativity, as you combine, complement and contrast the fascinating variations in form, growth habits, foliage shapes and colours, the beauty of flowers and fruits, as well as the often unique fragrances.

There is an Australian plant to suit every garden need. It's just waiting for you to find it.

Selecting suitable plants

Grevillea banksii

Eucalyptus leucoxylon

Allocasuarina verticillata

Hakea laurina

Leptospermum macrocarpum

One of the more important aspects of garden planning is to select plant species suitable to the conditions in your garden. We should aim to work with nature rather than against it as this will usually give a greater chance of success. If you are new to an area, talking to nursery staff and other gardeners in your neighbourhood can be most helpful. Reading gardening books and magazines which discuss particular plants and their requirements is also beneficial. This book and others in the Lothian Australian Garden series include a code which accompanies the plant descriptions, indicating some of a plant's major tolerances to garden conditions and there is further information about plants suitable for some of the more difficult situations on page 9.

If you can choose a plant that is naturally suited to each position available, you will be well on the way to achieving the type of success you seek in your garden. The plants are likely to grow well with little need for additional watering or fertilising, and healthy plants are usually more disease-resistant, minimising the need for attention.

Some species may require supplementary watering, so group these together to avoid the need to water the whole garden just for the sake of a few individual plants, and to avoid a detrimental effect on those species which prefer periods of dryness. Species with similar requirements for fertilisers should also be grouped together.

There are always likely to be particular plants you would like to grow even though you do not have the ideal situation for them. Improving the soil and raising the garden beds can help or you may consider growing the particular plant in a container. Cultivating plants in containers allows you to adjust the potting mixture to the specific requirements of each plant, and you can also move the container at particular times of the year to control the plant's exposure to sunshine and shade, frost or other climatic conditions.

Occasionally there will be plants which will seem to defy all your attempts to grow them with success. Some growers will simply accept this fact, and choose to grow something different, while others will relish the challenge, knowing that a greater sense of reward will come if they do eventually succeed.

Creating living pictures

Choosing a plant which is naturally suited to the position available is not all that is needed if you are to achieve the most pleasure from the garden. In planning a garden you have the opportunity to create living and changing pictures using plants and other garden features to complement or contrast with each other and with the buildings and other permanent fixtures on the site. It's important therefore to look at more than just the colourful flowers seen so often in books and on plant labels.

The major features to be considered initially are the size, form and growth habit of each plant. When a plant reaches its mature size, will it be suitable for the position you have given it? What effect will it have on other plants nearby? Will it still be possible to enjoy vistas from the windows of the house, walk down the pathways with ease, and have access to such facilities as electricity, gas and water meters? If it grows tall what effect will it have on the availability of sunshine for you and your neighbours? Most Australian plants respond well to regular pruning (as discussed on page 57), but plants which are misplaced and require constant attention to keep them within a desired size limit, may be seen as a nuisance after a few years, and it may be costly to have them removed.

There are Australian plants of every desired size and shape. With a little effort you will be able to find the ones most suited to your needs. The quality of a plant's foliage is often overlooked when planning or replanting a garden, but it is an extremely important contributor to the overall beauty of a garden year-round. We should aim to design an area so that pleasure can be gained from plants even when they are not in bloom.

Generally the beauty of foliage can be enhanced by arranging plants in pleasing combinations, and to provide contrasts in foliage colour and texture. There are many different shades of green, plus blue-greens, grey-greens, yellow-greens and even variegated plants with colour combinations. Many plants also have spectacular flushes of new growth with shades from soft pinks, silver greys, golds and reddish or rusty tones through to vivid reds. We can make use of these to provide pleasure when flowers aren't present.

The different textures and sizes of leaves can also add dimensions of interest and beauty to a garden. In small gardens they can often be made a focal point.

If you would prefer a more natural effect, try including some species with grass-like leaves. Grasses are an intricate part of the natural landscape, and several species are suitable for use in gardens to provide a soft, relaxing atmosphere. There are many other plants with grass-like foliage that have the additional advantage of producing colourful flowers. Some of these are listed in the section on Lilies and tufting plants on page 26.

Some plants have prickly foliage but should not be ignored because of their pungent tips. Such species can be used to advantage by placing them where they will guide or restrict foot traffic (of people or domestic pets), or they can be used to provide a refuge and nesting-place for native birds, safe from predators such as neighbourhood cats. Don't plant them close to pathways where they can constantly scratch legs or car paintwork.

The majority of garden plants are selected because of their flowers and whether you prefer subtle colour combinations or stronger contrasts in colour is largely a question of personal preference. If you are wanting species that will give a good combination of flower colour, make sure that their times of flowering will also coincide. Don't overlook the value of white or cream flowers in a garden. White, cream and yellow flowers can light up dark or drab sections of a garden, and they are excellent on grey, overcast days. Incidentally, plants with whitish or greyish foliage can play a very useful role beside driveways and pathways as they will reflect even minimum light at night and help to define the edge of the path.

A number of Australian plants are grown for their decorative fruits rather than for their flowers. Perhaps the best known are the mauve to purple-fruited Lilly pillys, which are species of *Acmena* and *Syzygium*. Many of the eucalypts have decorative fruits, including the Fuchsia Gum, *Eucalyptus forrestiana*, with yellow to bright orange or red buds and fruits which hang from the branches for several months. Other species with decorative fruits are marked by the reference ♂ in the plant descriptions.

Bird attracting plants in a garden can bring a further dimension of interest and beauty, and this is discussed further on page 17.

Combining Australian and introduced plants

Many gardeners want to mix Australian plants with plants from other countries. This is certainly possible but, as with any plants, you are more likely to have success if those with the same basic requirements are grouped together. It is generally unwise, for example, to try to grow a moisture-loving plant beside one from an arid region. The natural conditions may suit one but not the other, and any supplementary watering during dry periods is likely to affect the drought-tolerant species adversely.

When grouping different species together consider the plants' needs for fertilisers. It is important that they are compatible.

With these basic requirements in mind, there is no reason at all why Australian plants cannot be grown with exotic plants.

Many Australian eucalypts and other evergreen trees are useful for providing an overhead canopy under which some delicate exotic plants can thrive e.g. *Eucalyptus leucoxylon* ssp. *megalocarpa, E. scoparia* and *Hymenosporum flavum.* For formal gardens there is a wide range of Australian plants with suitable characteristics which will complement those from overseas. Many of them respond very well to pruning and regular clipping (see page 19), and a number can be trained for specific purposes.

In gardens which have an informal or perhaps wild or natural style the choices of compatible Australian plants are endless.

Plants for particular situations and uses

The provision of shade

Shade should be carefully considered in garden planning, because so many parts of Australia are subject to periods of extremely hot weather. A shaded area of the garden provides a pleasant place to sit and relax on a warm summer day, while giving protection from the harmful rays of direct sunshine. A healthy, well-developed shade tree can save several hundred dollars on the construction of verandahs, gazebos and similar structures.

Shade from strategically placed trees can protect walls and windows from the hot summer sun and make a tremendous difference to the internal temperature of buildings. Another cooling effect is provided by the fanning air movement through the foliage, and moisture evaporation from the leaves. Protection from cold winds provided by evergreen trees and shrubs during winter can also have a dramatic effect in reducing heating costs. See Windbreaks and screening plants, page 11.

On the negative side, too much shade in a garden can be detrimental to our enjoyment of the area, and will also restrict the number of other plants which can be grown, given the competition for light, soil moisture and nutrients. The planting of medium to large trees in a garden should be well planned. Make sure that, when mature, the tree will give the amount of shade you require. It should also be positioned so that the desired results are achieved in all seasons.

One important aspect to consider is the path of the sun across the sky at different times of the year. In summer it will be quite high, but much lower in winter. Therefore, if space permits, a large-growing evergreen tree planted at a correct distance from the house on the northern side will throw a shadow over the wall, windows and portion of the roof in summer, while allowing the warmth of the lower-angled winter sun to shine through beneath the branches. Some pruning of lower branches may be needed to allow more sunshine through. For mature trees it is best to remove these branches, especially if they are sizeable, gradually over a period of years.

Deciduous trees can also restrict summer sun and allow sunshine and warmth to penetrate during winter. There are relatively few Australian trees suitable for general cultivation, which lose all or most of their leaves during winter, but *Melia azedarach* var. *australasica* is one which will grow in a fairly wide range of conditions, and can be useful if you have sufficient space.

The chart lists a selection of Australian trees useful for the provision of shade, with most not growing too large for the average suburban garden. Other titles in the Lothian Australian Garden series — *Trees for Town and City Gardens* and *Shady Gardens*, will also be useful. If you are looking for some

Shade-providing trees

Plant names asterisked are discussed in detail in the text.

Acacia cognata 4–10m × 4–6m
  *pravissima
Acmena smithii 10–30m
*Agonis flexuosa
*Allocasuarina torulosa
*Angophora costata
Banksia serrata 10–20m
*Callistemon salignus
Callitris columellaris 15–20m
Castanospermum australe 10–30m
*Elaeocarpus reticulatus
Eucalyptus burdettiana 4–10m
  citriodora 15–30m
  crenulata 4–15m
  *leucoxylon ssp. *megalocarpa*
  *macrandra
  megacornuta 5–12m
  spathulata 6–12m
  torelliana 8–15m
Ficus rubiginosa 10–25m
Harpullia pendula 6–12m
*Hymenosporum flavum
Lophostemon confertus 10–35m
Macadamia intergrifolia 6–12m
Melaleuca leucadendron 15–25m
  *linariifolia
*Melia azedarach
  var. *australasica*
*Schefflera actinophylla
Syzygium cormiflorum 6–10m
  *paniculatum
Toona australis 15–25m
*Tristaniopsis laurina

taller-growing specimens or a wider range of species to choose from, additional books on Australian trees will be found under the heading of Further Reading, just before the Index.

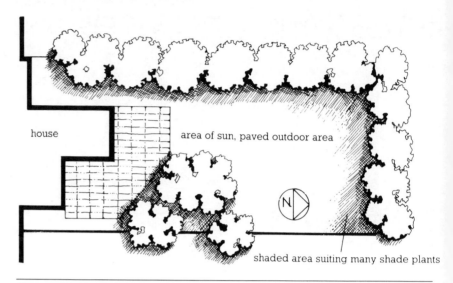

Creating shaded areas by judicious planting; plan of house and garden showing trees, shrubs, hedges and the effect of the sun to the north.

Plants for hot, sunny sites

Plant names asterisked are discussed in detail in the text.

Acacia argyrophylla 3–4m × 4–6m
  *boormanii
*Alyogyne huegelii
*Banksia ericifolia
Beaufortia sparsa 2–4m × 1–3m
*Billardiera ringens
*Callistemon 'Harkness'
  phoeniceus 2–4m × 3–5m
Calocephalus brownii 0.2–2m tall
*Cassia artemisioides
*Chamelaucium uncinatum
*Correa alba
  *pulchella
*Craspedia globosa
Dampiera rosmarinifolia
  to 0.5m × 2m
*Eremophila glabra
  maculata 0.5–3m × 1–3m
*Eucalyptus caesia
  *conferruminata
  *leucoxylon
  *macrandra
Frankenia pauciflora
  prostrate × 0.3m–1m
*Glischrocaryon behrii
*Grevillea juniperina
  *lavandulacea
  *'Poorinda Royal Mantle'
  *speciosa
  *thelemanniana
*Hakea laurina
Halgania cyanea 0.5m × 0.5–1m
*Helichrysum apiculatum
  *bracteatum
*Hemiandra pungens
*Hibbertia pedunculata
  *scandens
*Hymenosporum flavum
Kennedia beckxiana (climber)
*Kunzea baxteri
Leptospermum scoparium
  *macrocarpum
*Melaleuca decussata
  *fulgens
  *nesophila
  steedmanii 1.5–2.5m × 1–2m
*Melia azedarach var. australasica
*Myoporum parvifolium
*Pittosporum phylliraeoides
*Prostanthera aspalathoides
Rhagodia spinescens
  to 1m × 1.5–3m
*Templetonia retusa
*Thryptomene saxicola

Plants for hot, sunny sites

The variety of plants suitable for hot sites is extensive, and many of these need maximum sunshine in order to reach their potential. So if you have such a spot in your garden you could be halfway to growing some of the more spectacular flowering groundcovers, shrubs and trees.

If you wish to grow some of the plants listed in the chart it is imperative that you plan for their future development by selecting plants for the surrounding area which will not grow too tall and later begin to throw shade over what should be your hot, sunny garden.

For those who live in cooler regions who would dearly love to grow some of these floriferous plants which need maximum sunshine, there are some ways to make this easier.

A good location for these plants especially in temperate regions, is an area which has a wall, fence or other solid barrier on the southern side. This will tend to trap, absorb and radiate the sun's rays, extending the period of time when this garden area is warmer than the surrounds. If this is not an option, a dense planting of shrubs and trees will divert or soften the effect of cold winds. The positioning of these plants will depend on where your coldest winds enter the garden.

The establishment of plants in hot, sunny sites needs to be tackled carefully, otherwise losses of young plants may occur. Usually the best time for planting is in the cool of autumn. The ground will still be warm and advantageous for growth and the plants will settle in well to their new environment and will have developed a good root system by the end of spring so that they can cope with the extremes of the coming summer. If you are in an area which is prone to heavy frosts (unless you are planting frost tolerant species) it is probably wise to postpone planting until the danger of frost damage has passed. Planting in spring will mean you will need to be extremely diligent about a plant's watering requirements until it is established and can be left to its own resources.

Always be attentive to the water requirements of young plants in hot, sunny sites, because if they are developing quickly, lack of water will affect their growth. Regular watering may still be required over the first summer, so be vigilant. By this, I mean deep soak every 1–2 weeks, but plants may require even less regular attention. Never sprinkle the soil lightly as this will promote a fine network of roots near the surface where the soil is first to dry out through seepage and evaporation, and roots in this region will always be thirsting for more water.

I do recommend you use a mulch as this will help to retain moisture content in the soil, as well as reduce the fluctuations in soil temperature. Both aspects are beneficial for promoting plant growth. See page 56 for specific information on mulches.

In a windy location best results will usually be achieved if the plants are no larger than 30–50cm tall at the time of planting. Young plants usually acclimatise better to the conditions and, although their growth rate will possibly be slower than in a more favourable site, they should become much sturdier specimens than those over 1m tall at the time of planting.

Keep fertilisers to a minimum. Forced, overfed plants can be much weaker than those which develop at a slower rate, and any that become top-heavy are likely either to snap off or to blow over from the base.

Windbreaks and screening plants

Often we think of windbreak plants as only being associated with broad landscape or rural plantings. However, many smaller gardens also have a real need for wind protection, and often wind tunnels are formed or accentuated by the positioning of buildings, fences and other structures.

Windbreak plants have been found to have a noticeable impact on the temperatures of buildings to which they give protection. In winter it is possible to increase the temperature of a home or other building by providing a plant screen of evergreen foliage which will restrict the direct flow of cold air onto walls or window surfaces. There are also advantages in summer, as mentioned in the section on Shade trees (page 9).

Plant screens can also be used to direct foot traffic (of people or domestic animals), to provide privacy or to block an ugly view, or to give some protection from dust or, to a very limited degree, noise.

It is always best to plant species from several different height groupings at the same time for an effective screen, unless you will be training the plants into a hedge. Very few plants of tree size stay dense right to ground level, so as a tree matures and becomes leggy, the low level screening effect disappears. It is then very difficult to establish lower, shrubby species beneath the more established tree.

Relatively close planting can be undertaken if there is only limited space available. *Acacia boormanii*, *Banksia ericifolia*, *Jacksonia scoparia* and *Persoonia pinifolia*, are tall shrubs while for lower cover *Correa alba*, *Eriostemon myoporoides*, *Phebalium lamprophyllum* and *Westringia fruticosa* are well suited. All of these plants respond well to pruning and will develop well as hedges. In large-area plantings the plants can be positioned so that the wind is gradually taken in the desired direction, rather than being met by a dense vertical barrier. It is always best to create a windbreak which allows for some wind penetration.

Windbreaks and screening plants

Plant names asterisked are discussed in detail in the text.

Acacia (Wattles)
  cultriformis 2–5m × 2–5m
  howittii 4–8m × 3–6m
  *iteaphylla
  pravissima 4–8m × 4–8m
Baeckea virgata to 6m × 2–3m
*Banksia ericifolia
  *spinulosa
*Callistemon citrinus
  *salignus
  *viminalis
*Ceratopetalum gummiferum
*Correa alba
  *baeuerlenii
*Eriostemon myoporoides
*Eucalyptus conferruminata
  *macrandra
*Goodia lotifolia
Grevillea 'Ivanhoe' 2–5m × 3–5m
  lanigera to 3m × 5m
  *'Poorinda Constance'
  *thelemanniana shrubby forms
  *victoriae
Hakea petiolaris 3–6m × 2–4m
*Kunzea baxteri
*Leptospermum lanigerum
  parviflorum 3–8m × 3–6m
  *petersonii
*Melaleuca armillaris
  *decussata
  *diosmifolia
  *nesophila
*Westringia fruticosa
  'Wynyabbie Gem' 1.5–2.5m
    × 1.5–3m

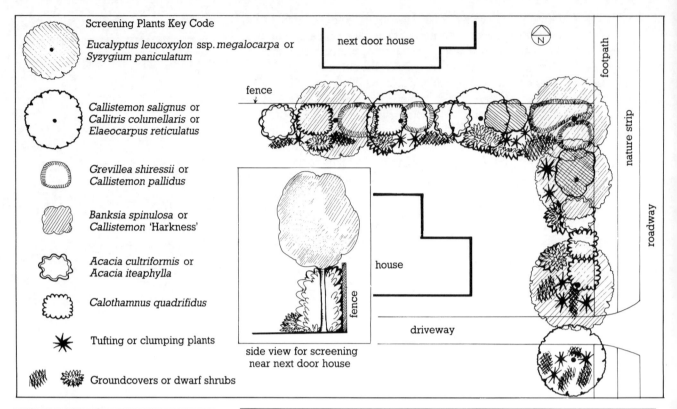

side view for screening
near next door house

Screening Plants Key Code

Eucalyptus leucoxylon ssp. megalocarpa or
Syzygium paniculatum

Callistemon salignus or
Callitris columellaris or
Elaeocarpus reticulatus

Grevillea shiressii or
Callistemon pallidus

Banksia spinulosa or
Callistemon 'Harkness'

Acacia cultriformis or
Acacia iteaphylla

Calothamnus quadrifidus

Tufting or clumping plants

Groundcovers or dwarf shrubs

A selection of frost-hardy plants

Plant names asterisked are discussed in detail in the text.

*Acacia pravissima
*Banksia ericifolia
  *marginata
  *spinulosa
*Bauera rubioides
*Boronia pinnata
*Callistemon pallidus
*Cassia artemisioides
*Correa alba
  *reflexa
*Crowea exalata
*Dianella tasmanica
*Epacris longiflora
*Eriostemon myoporoides
Eucalyptus coccifera 2–40m
  *leucoxylon
*Goodenia hederacea var. alpestris
*Grevillea alpina
  *juniperina
  *sericea
  *speciosa
*Melaleuca decussata
  *incana
  *thymifolia
*Micromyrtus ciliata
*Olearia phlogopappa
*Pratia pedunculata
*Prostanthera rotundifolia
*Pultenaea pedunculata
*Stylidium graminifolium
*Tetratheca thymifolia
*Viola hederacea

When planting to screen unwanted views, a combination of plants with differing mature heights is necessary. There is also no need to have a hedge-like appearance. The planting of small trees combined with tall or medium-sized shrubs will give good cover as well as the opportunity for flowers throughout most of the year. Additional dwarf shrubs or groundcovers such as species of Crowea, Dampiera and Grevillea will enable you to have colourful accents and tufting or clumping plants will provide different textures.

Planting in frost-prone areas

Those who garden in colder regions and have to contend with the vagaries of frosts may want to grow a wider range of species than those from the alpine areas of Australia which are, of course, highly tolerant of frost. Many species are only frost-tender when young, and protection during the first few seasons can be provided by a frame covered with shadecloth or hessian. Plastic is not recommended for this purpose. As plants mature, any new foliage may be burnt by heavy frosts, but the result is often simply an overall tip-pruning of the plant. See Tip pruning, page 57. Those species which are frost-tender through all stages of growth are best not grown in cold areas, unless in a very protected garden site or in a glasshouse, shadehouse or other similar structure.

Frost damage can be minimised if you make sure there is no thick layer of organic mulch against the base of a plant. When frozen mulch defrosts, there is a release of heat which can cause damage to plants at ground level.

Tissue damage may also be reduced if the foliage has a layer of water on it as it will act as an insulator before it becomes frosted overnight. Watering with a hose early in the morning can also help counteract burn damage to foliage and stems.

The plant descriptions on pages 20–45 include 🌡 which indicates those plants which will tolerate conditions with temperatures from 7°C down to −4°C, and in some cases much less. Plants coded 🌡 can suffer damage if temperatures fall below 7°C, and are therefore regarded as frost-tender.

Plants for exposed coastal situations

An exposed coastal position is one of the most difficult situations in which to establish a garden. Plants can suffer considerable damage from strong, salt-laden winds, and sometimes from direct salt spray.

At least one side of the house provides protection from the strongest winds and further walls and screens can be built but, if plants taller than the height of such walls are to be used, this will not always be effective. The plants will grow well until they reach the height of the wall. Then they will be exposed to the direct winds for the first time and unless you take additional precautions such as staking, they can become loose at the base or be blown over. You will have to start all over again.

A light screen, such as hessian or shadecloth, which allows some penetration of wind is preferable. The plant will grow a stronger trunk and better root development to cope with the situation, than if it has always relied on protection from the elements. Plants grown in an exposed position from an early age usually provide a better long-term result than advanced plants which must be staked or otherwise supported at the time of planting.

Many very desirable native garden plants grow naturally in coastal areas and are ideally suited to these conditions. Such plants can be used to form the basic framework of a coastal garden. If it is possible to establish a 'front line' planting of local species, a much greater range of plants can then be grown in the shelter provided. The 'front line' barrier should also allow for some wind penetration.

'Front line' plants will usually grow more slowly than the same species planted elsewhere, as frequent burning of soft, new leaf growth by the salt-laden winds will have the same effect as regular tip-pruning. But slower overall growth is both normal and desirable under the conditions, as sturdier plants will result.

Soil salinity caused by salt spray deposited by coastal winds over many years can occur in coastal areas.

Salinity is also found in flat land where the water-table lies close to the surface and evaporation of moisture causes a slow but steady build-up of the salts which are left behind.

One of the main, and very practical, ways in which saline soils can be restored to fertility is through the planting of as many salt-tolerant plants as possible. These help by lowering the water table, so that upper-level salts can then be flushed through the soil by future rains. Planting should begin on the upper slopes of the affected areas, where there is the greatest chance of good growth. Then gradually introduce more plants at lower levels.

In coastal areas some non-indigenous Australian plants and exotic plants have become weeds by adapting very well and spreading quickly to the disadvantage of the local plants. If planting in coastal areas, where well-established native vegetation is present, guard against such problems by carefully choosing the plants you introduce.

Plants for steep slopes and embankments

Erosion is often thought of as belonging primarily to broad-scale landscaping or rural sites. However, many home gardens include embankments which have been created by excavations for buildings, driveways or roads. Unless these slopes are appropriately landscaped, the topsoil will wash down onto footpaths or roadways. In most cases the hard surface of the sloping cut area, as well as the fill area may be a mass of large, solid clay lumps.

Before planting, there is usually need for some landscaping construction.

Plants for exposed coastal situations

Plant names asterisked are discussed in detail in the text.

†	Tolerates moderate exposure
††	Will tolerate fully exposed conditions
0	Suitable for dry, sandy, saline soils
00	Suitable for wet or swampy saline soils.

*Acacia ligulata 2–5m × 4–7m	†0
*pravissima	†
sophorae 2–8m × 4–10m	††
*suaveolens	††
*Actinotus helianthi Flannel Flower	†
*Agonis flexuosa	†
*Allocasuarina verticillata	††
Angophora hispida 3–10m	††
*Anigozanthos flavidus	†
*Astartea fascicularis	†
*Banksia ericifolia	†
*integrifolia	††
*Callistemon 'Harkness'	†
*pallidus	†
*salignus	†0
speciosus 2–4m × 1–3m	††
Calocephalus brownii Cushion Bush 20cm–2m tall	††
*Calothamnus quadrifidus	†
*Chamelaucium uncinatum	†
*Clematis microphylla	†
*Correa alba	††
*pulchella	†
*reflexa	†
*Darwinia citriodora	†
*Eucalyptus conferruminata	†
*leucoxylon ssp.megalocarpa	†
Frankenia pauciflora Southern Sea-heath to 0.3m × 1m	††0
*Grevillea juniperina	†
*thelemanniana	†
*Hardenbergia comptoniana	†
*Helichrysum bracteatum	†
*Hibbertia scandens	†
*Kunzea baxteri	†
*pomifera	††0
*Lagunaria patersonii	††
*Lasiopetalum macrophyllum	††
Leptospermum laevigatum 3–6m	††
*Melaleuca armillaris	†00
*decussata	†00
*diosmifolia	††
*fulgens	†
*nesophila	†
*thymifolia	†
*Myoporum parvifolium	††
*Patersonia occidentalis	†
*Pimelea ferruginea	††
*Templetonia retusa	††
*Westringia fruticosa	††

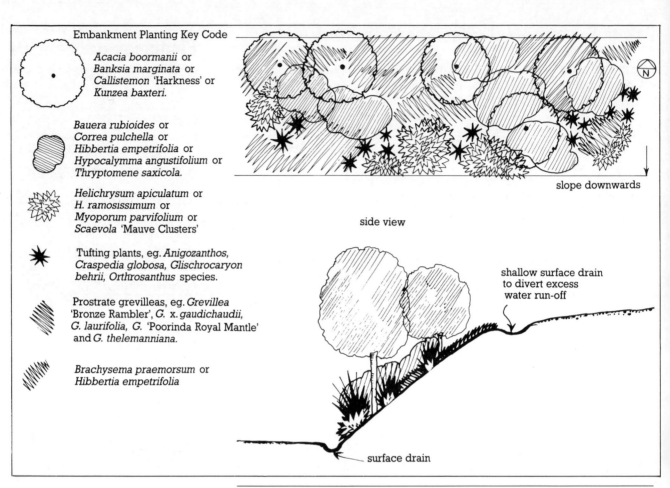

Embankment Planting Key Code

Acacia boormanii or
Banksia marginata or
Callistemon 'Harkness' or
Kunzea baxteri.

Bauera rubioides or
Correa pulchella or
Hibbertia empetrifolia or
Hypocalymma angustifolium or
Thryptomene saxicola.

Helichrysum apiculatum or
H. ramosissimum or
Myoporum parvifolium or
Scaevola 'Mauve Clusters'

Tufting plants, eg. Anigozanthos,
Craspedia globosa, Glischrocaryon
behrii, Orthrosanthus species.

Prostrate grevilleas, eg. Grevillea
'Bronze Rambler', G. x. gaudichaudii,
G. laurifolia, G. 'Poorinda Royal Mantle'
and G. thelemanniana.

Brachysema praemorsum or
Hibbertia empetrifolia

slope downwards

side view

shallow surface drain
to divert excess
water run-off

surface drain

Embankment plantings are extremely varied. Some people opt for a simple treatment by using the same type of plant for the whole area. This can be fine if all plants develop well, but is often not satisfactory when some plants die. A combination of plants with differing textures, form and size allows for a variation in plant performance and can also provide variation in enjoyment as plants flower at different times.

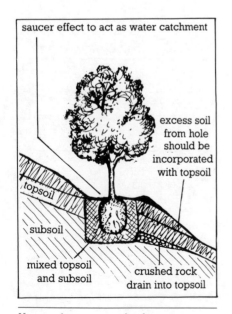

saucer effect to act as water catchment

excess soil
from hole
should be
incorporated
with topsoil

topsoil

subsoil

mixed topsoil
and subsoil

crushed rock
drain into topsoil

How to plant on an embankment

Some slopes are very steep and will not be stable without some form of support. Brick or rock walling, timber, or perhaps a combination of these materials may be necessary to shore up the slope. These must be constructed strongly enough to withstand the considerable pressures they will face from the soil behind the wall. You may need some professional help to design and/ or build an adequate retaining wall. Crushed rock and an agricultural drain near the inner base of the wall are often also required. For further information on these points see *Building for the Garden*, pages 17–25.

On gentle slopes a common practice is to use rocks. If they are used sympathetically and placed to look as though they actually belong there, a wonderful effect can be achieved. All too often rocks are simply placed on the surface or in shallow depressions, quite unlike anything seen in nature. Rocks usually have one or more surfaces which you should exploit. Select the best sides or surfaces of the rock to be retained above ground level. and *half*-bury it. Not only will it look more natural, it will also be less likely to move downhill causing possible damage to plants, property or even humans or family pets.

An over-use of rocks can create a jarring, cluttered effect, whereas a simple treatment with a limited number of well-placed rocks of varying sizes that complement each other can provide a pleasant spaciousness.

Heavy rains will cause erosion around recently placed rocks, so it is important to keep an eye on the slope so that you can control any erosion during this settling period.

The selection of plants for slopes and embankments depends upon a number of factors. These include:
- What direction does the embankment face?
- Is the soil moist or dry for the greatest part of the year?
- How much sun does the area receive?
- Is the area subject to strong winds?
- What depth of topsoil is there?

Often there is no topsoil. If the slope is very steep, it is usually best to plant trailing plants at the top, and as they grow peg the stems down using wire pegs.

For gently sloping embankments with negligible topsoil it is best to use small plants from shallow containers. This will overcome the need to dig large deep holes which can act as water-gathering sumps and cause problems in growth. Larger plants can be used when you have plenty of topsoil or if you can provide adequate drainage from below the base of the plant. Young, small plants, however, are usually able to develop a strong root system which penetrates the subsoil and they become sturdy with age.

On embankments of filled soil or clay, good growth can be gained without too much despair. Three to six months after completion of the embankment some consolidation should have occurred, and yet the soil will not be too compacted. (Compaction of the soil will limit plant growth.) The addition of gypsum at 1–1.5kg per square metre for the length of the embankment before planting can help to improve friability of the soil, which promotes better growth.

Groundcovering plants which are self-layering or suckering are an excellent choice for embankments as they can help lessen the rapidity of water-flow down a slope and thus restrict erosion. But don't neglect to use taller plants, as often their roots will also help to stabilise the embankment and a pleasing visual effect can be gained by using plants of differing heights. This is worth considering if you have a long embankment.

Applying a water penetrable mulch, such as wood chips or pinebark, is beneficial if it can be anchored or held on the slope. There are a number of woven plastic mulching materials in rolls which can be used, and these should be put in place before you plant. Access through the material is achieved by making two cuts in the shape of a cross. Properly applied mulches 5–7cm deep can help to reduce weed growth. Any weeds should be removed while they are very small and as soon as they are noticed. This will help prevent you removing large amounts of soil on the roots of any weeds. You should aim for as little disturbance of mulch and soil as possible on slopes and embankments.

Plants for narrow situations

If you have a very narrow garden bed, how often do you find that every plant of 1m or more will be much too wide for the position? Narrow, upright Australian plants are much less common than those which have a similar or greater width than height. However, there are some to choose from, and a selection of these has been listed here.

Bear in mind that by gradually removing side branches that are flush with the trunk from large shrubs or trees at an early stage, and continuing to do so as the plant matures, it is possible to encourage an upper storey of foliage on a clean, narrow trunk. A trunk without side branches has very little width, yet

Plants suitable for growing on steep slopes and embankments

Plant names asterisked are discussed in detail in the text.

Acacia acinacea 0.5–2.5m × 2–4m
  *boormanii
  *pravissima 'Golden Carpet'
Banksia blechnifolia to 0.5m × 2–4m
Billardiera scandens (climber)
*Blechnum minus
Boronia crenulata 0.6–1m × 0.5–1m
*Brachysema praemorsum
  sericeum 0.2–1m × 1–4m
*Callistemon citrinus
  *'Harkness'
  *pallidus
  *viminalis
*Cassia artemisioides
Chorizema cordatum 1–2m × 1–2m
*Correa decumbens
  *'Dusky Bells'
Culcita dubia (Rainbow Fern)
  0.5–1.5m tall. Spreading.
*Dampiera linearis
  purpurea 1–1.5m × 0.5–2m
  rosmarinifolia to 0.5m × 2m
Darwinia taxifolia ssp. macrolaena
  0.1–1m × 1–2m
*Doodia aspera
Eremophila serpens
  prostrate × 1.5–3m
*Eriostemon myoporoides
Goodenia lanata prostrate × 60cm–1.5m
*Grevillea curviloba
  × *gaudichaudii
  *laurifolia
  longifolia 2.5–5m × 3–6m
  *'Poorinda Royal Mantle'
  synapheae 0.2–1.5m × 1–2.5m
  *thelemanniana
Halgania cyanea 50cm × 0.5–1m
*Hardenbergia violacea
Hibbertia aspera 0.1–2.5m × 1–1.5m
  *scandens
*Kennedia eximia
  *macrophylla
  *rubicunda
*Kunzea pomifera
Leptospermum scoparium 'Horizontalis'
  0.5–1m × 2–4m
Melaleuca pulchella 1–1.5m × 1.5–2m
  wilsonii 1–2.5m × 1–3m
*Myoporum parvifolium
  viscosum 1–2m × 1–2m
Nephrolepis cordifolia (Fish-bone Fern)
  to 1m × 2m
*Polystichum proliferum
*Pultenaea pedunculata
Rhagodia spinescens (Hedge Saltbush)
  to 1m × 1.5–3m
*Scaevola striata
Symphionema montanum 0.3–1m
  × 0.3–1m
Thomasia purpurea 1–2m × 1–2m
Xanthosia rotundifolia 30–50cm × 1–2m

Plants for narrow situations

Plant names asterisked are discussed in detail in the text.

Acacia boormanii
Agonis juniperina (Juniper Myrtle)
    5–10m × 3–5m
Anigozanthos (Kangaroo Paws)
Baeckea virgata to 6m × 2–3m
Beaufortia decussata 2–3m × 1–2m
Boronia deanei to 2m × 0.5–1.5m
    denticulata to 2.5m × 1.5m
        heterophylla
        megastigma
Callistemon viminalis
Callitris oblonga 2–8m × 1–3m
Calytrix tetragona
Cordyline petiolaris 2–7m × 1–3m
    stricta 2–5m × 0.5–1.5m
Correa schlechtendalii 0.5–2.5m × 1–2m
Craspedia globosa
Dianella tasmanica
Diplarrena moraea
Epacris impressa
    reclinata
Grevillea jephcottii 2–2.5m × 1.5–2m
    sericea
Homoranthus darwinioides
Hymenosporum flavum
Isopogon anethifolius Conebush
    1.5–3m × 1–2m
Jacksonia scoparia 3–5m × 1.5–3m
Leptospermum petersonii
    polygalifolium 2–8m × 1.5–5m
Melaleuca micromera 2–2.5m × 1–2m
    squamea 1–3m × 1–1.5m
Orthrosanthus multiflorus
Patersonia occidentalis
Templetonia retusa
Tetratheca thymifolia

Often when dealing with narrow sites we opt for similar plants, when really there is plenty of opportunity to create a strip of interesting textures, forms and floral displays. Climbers are worth considering to cover fences and soften their harsh lines. One or two trees can provide height and when trained up on trunks they only take up room for their trunks. Don't neglect to include clumping or tufting plants such as kangaroo paws, dianellas or morning flags. The inclusion of shrubs which have a narrow growth habit, or those that respond well to pruning, will add variation too. The odd groundcover will fill in any bare spots as well as camouflaging the harsh edges of paths or driveways.

an upper canopy to provide shade or a visual screen can still be achieved. If this method is used, be careful not to force the plant by excessive use of fertilisers, or it may become top-heavy and possibly blow over in strong winds.

A number of plants that would normally be too large for narrow sites, but which respond well to pruning or clipping, should also be considered as they may be very suitable for your requirements. If you wish to have a hedge-like growth for your narrow sites, don't always feel obliged to use the same plant. You can create some interesting and attractive plantings using different species, especially if you select plants with variations in foliage textures and flowering times. See also Windbreaks and screening plants, on page 11.

Climbing plants can also be very useful in narrow garden situations, and these are grouped together in the plant descriptions section on pages 40–1.

An enticing entrance to a front door but the garden also implores you to come and explore the combination of groundcovers, shrubs and trees. Pink flowers of various hues are provided by *Boronia muelleri* 'Sunset Serenade' (pale pink), *Boronia serrulata* (in pot), and *Thomasia grandiflora*. The dainty white-flowered variant of *Hardenbergia comptoniana* adorns the pergola post. The boulder makes an excellent seat for observing the nectar-feeding birds which come to visit the flowers of *Eucalyptus leucoxylon* ssp. *megalocarpa* above.

Whites, blues and mauves adorn either side of a gravelled path. The flannel flower, *Actinotus helianthi* is in the foreground with the white of *Leptospermum brevipes* in the background. *Brachyscome multifida* 'Breakoday' on the left hand side has flowers all the year whilst on the right *Dampiera linearis* has its display during late spring and early summer.

ABOVE A pleasing combination of different plant shapes and textures with the taller shrubs screening another part of the garden, thus helping to provide an element of surprise as you pass by. The bright yellow of *Acacia myrtifolia* is complemented by *Conostylis candicans*, the smaller tufting plant in the foreground, while the golden yellow of a bush pea contrasts with the mauves and pinks of other smaller plants.

BELOW Simplicity can make a valuable impact in a small garden. *Leptospermum rotundifolium* 'Lavender Queen' nestles below a taller *Grevillea* and beside a boulder with *Spyridium parvifolium* 'Austraflora Nimbus' hugging the ground with its spreading green foliage.

Fragrant flowers and foliage

Many plants are renowned for the fragrance of their flowers or leaves. Others have more subtle aromas which contribute to the overall fragrance enjoyed on entering their section of the garden. Growing fragrant plants in a garden is another way of enhancing the pleasure to be gained from the area.

Usually when we think of fragrant Australian flowers one of the first species to come to mind is the Brown Boronia, *Boronia megastigma*. It has been grown for many years for the cut-flower trade and sold by florists in Australia and in other parts of the world. Some unfortunate people cannot appreciate the brown boronia perfume because their olfactory nerves do not respond. People can react like this to other fragrant plants too. It is similar to the different ways in which people react to certain food tastes.

There are many Australian plants well worth growing for their floral fragrances, and a selection of these is provided in the chart.

While fragrant flowers bloom for only a portion of the year, aromatic foliage on evergreen plants gives continued enjoyment. The fragrance tends to be released on warm to hot days, after heavy rain or hail, or when the foliage is brushed or crushed. When planning a garden always make sure that you have some fragrant-foliaged plants next to a path or within arm's length so that people will brush past the foliage or can gently run their hands along a leafy branch to release the fragrance.

Eucalypts are well known for their fragrant oils. Blue mallee is the oil most commonly available in shops, but there are also lemon scented eucalypts, and several species with a peppermint fragrance to the leaves. Height can be a problem with some of these trees, which grow to be quite tall and are not always suited to suburban gardens. Further information on different eucalypts can be found in the many reference books devoted entirely to this genus.

Australia is also renowned for the foliage fragrances provided by the genus *Prostanthera*, or mint bushes. Several are listed in the plant descriptions on page 17, and they will supply a showy display of flowers in addition to their delightful fragrances. *Backhousia citriodora* is hard to surpass for the clear lemon fragrance of the leaves. The perfume remains even after the leaves have dried and fallen from the plant, so don't clean them all up but leave them to be crushed when walked on.

The chart lists some of the more commonly grown and renowned Australian plants with fragrant flowers or foliage, and further species can be found by looking for the symbol 🍃 in the plant descriptions on pages 20–45.

Plants with fragrant flowers or foliage

Plant names asterisked are discussed in detail in the text.

fo = has fragrant foliage
fl = has fragrant flowers

Acacia iteaphylla	fl
*suaveolens	fl
Alpinia caerulea Native Ginger	
1–3m × 1–2m	fl
Backhousia citriodora Lemon-scented	
Myrtle 3–20m	fo
Boronia floribunda 1–1.5m	fl/fo
*megastigma	fl
*muelleri	fl/fo
*pinnata	fo
Calytrix aurea 1–2m	fl
*Cassia artemisioides	fl
Chamelaucium ciliatum 50cm–1m	fo
*Crinum pendunculatum	fl
*Cymbidium madidum	fl
*Darwinia citriodora	fo
*Dendrobium falcorostrum	fl
*speciosum	fl
Eucalyptus citriodora Lemon-scented	
Gum 15–30m	fo
*Hardenbergia comptoniana	fl
*Homoranthus darwinioides	fo
*Hoya australis	fl
*Hymenosporum flavum	fl
Jacksonia scoparia 3–5m	fl
Jasminum aemulum climber	fl
*suavissimum	fl
*Leptospermum petersonii	fo
*Micromyrtus ciliata	fo
Prostanthera, Mint Bushes	
*ovalifolia	fo
rotundifolia 1.5–2.5m	fo
Stackhousia monogyna to 40cm	fl

Bird-attracting plants

In addition to having a rich and varied flora, Australia also has a wide range of fascinating native birds which can add a great deal of interest and beauty to domestic gardens. Many of these birds rely on flowers and fruits of native plants as a food source.

If we wish to attract these wonderful creatures to our gardens the three basic requirements of food, water and shelter need to be considered. If we can provide what the birds need they will visit and some may even become residents and perhaps nest there.

Different birds seek their food from different sources. There are the honey-eaters which gather nectar from the flowers, and they also need insects as a very important part of their diet. There are insect-eaters, including small birds such as robins and wrens, which seek out insects. Seed-eaters such as finches look for the small seeds of grasses and other plants, while members

Bird-attracting plants

Plant names asterisked are discussed in detail in the text.

N = Nectar
S = Seeds & Fruits

Most flowering plants attract insects, which are also an important source of food for all birds.

Acacia (Wattles)	
myrtifolia 1–3m × 2–3m	S
pycnantha 3–10m × 2–6m	S
*Angophora costata	N
*Anigozanthos flavidus	N
Austromyrtus dulcis (Midgen Berry) 50cm–1.5m × 1–2m	S
*Banksia ericifolia	N
*Callistemon citrinus	N
*'Harkness'	N
subulatus 2–4m × 2–4m	N
*viminalis	N
Castanospermum australe (Black Bean) 10–30m × 5–12m	N
*Conostylis bealiana	N
*Correa glabra	N
*'Mannii'	N
*reflexa	N
Darwinia taxifolia ssp. macrolaena 0.1–1m × 1–2m	N
*Epacris longiflora	N
*Eucalyptus caesia	N
*leucoxylon ssp. megalocarpa	N
*macrandra	N
megacornuta 5–12m tall	N
sideroxylon 10–30m tall	N
torelliana 8–15m tall	N
Euodia elleryana 12–20m tall	N
*Grevillea alpina	N
arenaria 1.5–1.5m tall	N
*× gaudichaudii	N
jephcottii 2–2.5m tall	N
*juniperina	N
*longistyla hybrid	N
*'Poorinda Constance'	N
*'Poorinda Queen'	N
robusta 10–25m tall	N
shiressii 3–8m × 2–6m	N
*thelemanniana	N
*victoriae	N
*Homoranthus darwinioides	N
*Melaleuca hypericifolia	N
lateritia 2–4m tall	N
Metrosideros queenslandica to 10m tall	N
Neolitsea dealbata to 10m tall	S
*Schefflera actinophylla	N/S
*Stenocarpus sinuatus	N
Syzygium australe to 10m tall	S
cormiflorum to 10m tall	S
*paniculatum	S
*Telopea speciosissima	N
*Xanthostemon chrysanthus	N

of the parrot family eat larger seeds and fruits, but can also help to control gall insects by eating their larvae. Some of the larger birds seen in gardens, such as magpies and kookaburras, will help the gardener by devouring caterpillars, cockchafer grubs and other small creatures.

It is generally easier to encourage the smaller birds such as honey-eaters, seed-eaters and insect-eaters to visit gardens in rural, suburban and city areas. These feathered friends are a great pleasure to watch but they also help the gardener as natural pest controllers. We are now, thankfully, much more aware of the dangers of indiscriminate use of pesticides, some of which can have devastating long-term effects, including the wiping out of predator insects such as ladybirds which are excellent for controlling various scale insects. We need to encourage birds to be our pest controllers. They may not entirely rid our gardens of insect pests (and if they did there would not be food for them at a later date). A small insect population in a garden is part of the balance of nature. Some caterpillars can even be useful as they act as natural pruning agents, helping to promote sideshoots and resulting in more densely foliaged plants.

Small birds such as thornbills and pardalotes are certainly severe on scale and other small insects such as aphids. Larger caterpillars may be eaten by wattlebirds and magpies. Most people abhor sawfly caterpillars which congregate in a seething mass during the day, only to disperse and devour foliage at night; however, black-faced cuckoo shrikes, currawongs and red wattlebirds find them tasty.

There is a wide range of plants which produce either abundant nectar, or seeds which attract native birds, and some of these are included in the plant descriptions on pages 20–45 indicated by.

By growing some of these plants you will make a positive contribution to increasing bird habitat and reducing the need for using environmentally unfriendly products.

Supplementary feeding can be provided by the use of seed trays or bottle feeders if you wish, but this should be supplementary only to a natural source of food provided through plants. The plants are not likely to run out of nectar if you go away on holidays as a liquid feeder bottle may do!

If you wish birds to be regular visitors to the garden, it is important that you provide a constant source of water for them. A specially constructed bird bath will fulfil this role, as will a small pond, or even a shallow dish of suitable size. It is important that any such structure not be located where neighbourhood cats are able to attack the birds as they drink or bathe.

Shelter, the third important feature in attracting birds to a garden, can be provided for small birds by dense, shrubby plants. By planting three or more plants with prickles, or sharply pointed leaves, in close proximity, a suitable nesting site can be provided where the birds will feel secure against predators. Nesting boxes can also be constructed or purchased, and these will often be used by members of the parrot family and other birds such as kookaburras. Dead trees which have hollows suitable for nesting are usually removed in residential areas, leaving a shortage of suitable nesting sites.

Hedging, topiary, pruning, pleaching and bonsai

Australian plant growers have in the past tended to allow their plants to develop naturally, rather than manipulate them to conform to particular shapes as is traditional in much formal European gardening. However, for those interested in a more formal garden style there are certainly Australian species which can be grown in this way.

A wide range of species make attractive low garden hedges, including species of *Baeckea* (low species), *Bauera, Boronia, Crowea, Cryptandra, Eriostemon, Grevillea, Phebalium, Pimelea* and *Westringia*.

For taller hedges species of *Backhousia, Callistemon, Calothamnus, Grevillea, Leptospermum, Melaleuca* and *Syzygium* respond well to regular clipping and can provide a dense cover.

Pleached hedges and walkways were popular in England during the Tudor period. Lower side branches of the selected plants are removed so that a clean straight trunk supporting a canopy of upper growth remains. Such hedges are useful where a tall screen is needed in a small space, or to provide an upper-level screen whilst still allowing you to see through the trunks. Pleached trees make a very pleasant covered and shaded walkway. Very little work has been done using Australian plants in this way but many species are suitable. Some with ornamental trunks and barks which are so much a part of the Australian flora are *Acmena smithii, Leptospermum petersonii, Melaleuca linariifolia, Melaleuca styphelioides, Syzygium* species, and *Tristaniopsis laurina*.

Syzygium paniculatum

Topiary involves the regular trimming of shrubs into ornamental shapes, and in overseas countries *Syzygium paniculatum* is used quite extensively for this purpose. (For further information on general pruning techniques, see page 57.)

Plaiting and intertwining of branches to produce patterns or shapes is used with exotic species such as *Lagerstroemia* to produce interesting and dramatic effects. Some Chinese gardeners are very expert at this. Some of the slender-branched species of *Leptospermum*, e.g. *Leptospermum brevipes* and *Leptospermum petersonii*, should be suitable. Others which are worth trialling include *Baeckea behrii, Baeckea virgata, Billardiera* spp., *Chamelaucium* spp., *Darwinia citriodora, Hardenbergia violacea* and *Pandorea* spp., but the scene is wide open for experimentation.

Bonsai, or Penjing, is another form of specialised horticulture where plants are regularly pruned and wired to restrict their size and produce a specimen of a desired shape. A large number of Australian plants are now cultivated as bonsai specimens, including species of *Allocasuarina, Banksia, Brachychiton, Casuarina, Eucalyptus, Ficus, Leptospermum, Nothofagus* and *Podocarpus*.

Enthusiasts have proven that the basic principles and practices of bonsai cultivation can be equally effective with Australian plants, and specialist bonsai societies exist in all Australian states.

Many Australian plants are grown very successfully in containers of various sizes without resorting to bonsai techniques. By growing plants in pots you can have a wide variety of dwarf to small plants which can be transported to any part of your garden where you feel they will provide a visual lift. The subject of container plants is beyond the scope of this book however, *The New Australian Plants for Small Gardens and Containers* by my wife Gwen is worth reading.

Leptospermum laevigatum

Plants to grow

Code Key

Light levels

✦ Light shade or semi-shade

✸ Full shade

☼ Sun

Temperature

🌡 Cool, frost tolerant

🌡 Warm, minimum 7°C at night, does not tolerate frost

Water requirements

◊◊ Moist, but well drained

◊ Withstands periods of dryness

◊◊ Tolerates wet or poorly-drained conditions

Special features

❀ Flower

◔ Fruit

🖋 Foliage

⚲ Perfume

▯ Bark

🐦 Bird attracting

This section provides detailed descriptions of over 250 Australian plants. Plants described in this section are grouped in the following categories: Annuals, Groundcovers, Lilies and tufting plants, Orchids, Ferns, Shrubs, Climbers, Trees. A code key has been used to provide a concise reference to their cultivation requirements.

Annuals

And other plants with short life spans

Annuals are plants which germinate, grow to maturity, flower, and produce seed, usually within one year.

There are a number of annual plants native to Australia, and often large expanses of the drier regions become covered with these 'wildflowers' after heavy soaking rains. A large proportion are members of the daisy family. Some are everlastings and these are increasingly popular as fresh or dried cut-flowers.

In garden cultivation, annuals require different treatment to trees and shrubs. Their growth is rapid, and their need for moisture and nutrients is correspondingly high during this period. Good growth is often achieved in nutrient-rich garden soils in which compost or animal manures have been incorporated. Water-soluble fertilisers, which are immediately absorbed by the plants, can also be used. Long-term, slow-release fertilisers are generally not suited to annuals but those with a 3–4 month release are useful.

Annuals can be used in a garden to provide a colourful display during their flowering period. Wonderful and exciting combinations in massed plantings or informal drifts are readily achieved. Their beauty usually compensates for the fact that they are short-lived. If conditions are suitable, they will often self-seed in the garden, with new plants reappearing in subsequent seasons.

Annuals are also excellent for newly planted gardens where shrubs and trees are not very large and are yet to make an impact.

In addition to plants which are strictly annual in nature, there is a wider range of species with limited, short-term life spans. Often they are best cultivated as annuals or biennials, then replaced with new specimens propagated from seed or cuttings as the parent plants lose vigour and become less attractive. Included in this group are flannel flowers, *Actinotus* species, and some of the small kangaroo paws.

Actinotus helianthi
Flannel Flower

This species is not strictly annual, but a herbaceous to somewhat woody plant of 0.5–1.5m × 0.5–1m, with soft, grey, deeply lobed leaves. Plants flower over a long period, with a peak in spring to summer. The flowers are to around 8cm across, and daisy-like, with flannel-like bracts of white to cream tipped with green. Will commonly self-seed if conditions are favourable. Is cultivated as a cut-flower.

Actinotus helianthi

Anigozanthos humilis
Cat's Paw

A small, clump-forming plant, with strap-like leaves to around 20cm long. The flowers are produced on stems to around 50cm tall, mainly during winter and spring. They can be cream, yellow to orange or pink to red. The species is not a true annual, but following flowering, plants become deciduous and may or may not re-emerge during the following autumn. To stimulate plant vigour and increase the number of plants being grown, propagation by division can be undertaken as new autumn growth develops. Several other *Anigozanthos* or kangaroo paw species and cultivars also benefit from regular root division.

Brachyscome iberidifolia
Swan River Daisy

This species grows to around 50cm tall × 0.3–1m across, and is best grown as an annual. During spring to summer there is a colourful display of small, daisy flowers which can be white, blue or purple with yellow centres.

Clianthus formosus
Sturt's Desert Pea

A prostrate or trailing plant of 1–4m across, with soft, grey-green foliage. It is the floral emblem of South Australia, and the spectacular red or red with black pea-flowers can be produced over a long period from winter to late summer. Likes a warm to hot, very well-drained situation. Although often living more than one year in its natural habitat, it is usually intolerant of cold, wintry conditions and summer humidity, and in situations where these conditions are experienced, it is best grown as an annual.

Helichrysum
Everlastings; Straw Flowers

This genus belongs to the daisy family and includes some species which are annuals, and others which are perennials. **Helichrysum bracteatum** is a variable species with both annual and perennial selections commonly cultivated. Those forms which are annuals usually grow with upright habit to 0.5–1.5m tall. The papery everlasting daisies seen mainly in spring and summer, can be white, yellow, deep gold or pink. Further information in this species is contained in the section on Shrubs on page 36. **Helichrysum cassinianum** is a smaller plant growing around 30–50cm tall. Its small, pink, everlasting flowers are produced in clusters.

Helipterum
Everlastings; Sunrays

This genus includes around 60 Australian species, although some may be re-classified following botanical revision. All have papery flower-heads, and many are extremely decorative in gardens, and also widely grown for cut-flower use. They flower best in a warm, well-drained situation. **Helipterum floribundum** grows to around 60cm tall, and its white daisies with yellow centres are produced mainly in winter and spring. **Helipterum humboldtianum** also grows to around 60cm tall, with clusters of bright yellow flowers seen mainly during spring. **Helipterum manglesii** is of similar height to the previous two species, and produces a showy display of pink, papery daisies during spring and summer. Although still widely available from nurseries and seed suppliers under this name, its correct name is now *Rhodanthe manglesii*. **Helipterum roseum** can grow to around 1m tall. It is widely grown as a showy garden plant, and by the cut-flower trade. White or pink everlasting daisies of around 4cm across provide an eye-catching display during spring and summer.

Trachymene coerulea
Rottnest Daisy

This annual species of which seed is widely available, is commonly grown as a cut-flower. It reaches a height of up to 1m, and during spring to summer has small, soft blue flowers, produced in heads of up to 6cm across.

Trachymene coerulea

Brachyscome multifida

Groundcovers

There are many very attractive, prostrate or low-growing Australian plants, and a selection of these is provided here. Groundcovers can be very useful in a garden as they can, to some extent help as a living mulch to protect the soil from the heat of the sun, provide a sheltered environment for the root systems of other species, and prevent some moisture loss from the topsoil through evaporation. They can also be of value in reducing compaction of the soil from rain and overhead sprinklers. Groundcovers can limit weed growth in a garden, although they should not be expected to eliminate strong infestations of perennial weed species.

Groundcover plants should, if possible, be included in a garden planting at the same time as other taller species. This will allow them to develop together, rather than having to compete later, often in shady conditions, with other plants which are already well established.

Acacia pravissima 'Golden Carpet'
Ovens Wattle, prostrate form

This cultivar selection spreads horizontally, and can grow to 3–5m across, with a height of around 30cm. It is excellent for large areas or embankment planting. It bears masses of bright yellow flower-balls during spring. Some other prostrate variants of **Acacia pravissima** are now becoming available.

Brachyscome multifida
Cut-leaf Daisy

A clump-forming plant with a height of 20–60cm, growing to 1–1.5m across. It has small, soft-petalled daisy flowers of white, pink or mauve to bluish purple, which can be produced almost non-stop throughout the year. The selection 'Breakoday' is particularly good and the flowers are bluish purple with a yellow centre. Plants are rejuvenated by hard pruning in autumn or early spring.

Brachysema praemorsum

There are several prostrate *Brachysema* species. This one is readily recognised by the leaves which appear as if the tip has been cut off. It grows up to 1m tall, with a spread of 1–3m. The cream pea-flowers produced from winter through to summer, deepen to a reddish colour as they mature. The selection 'Bronze Butterfly' has dark coppery green leaves. Additional prostrate brachysemas include **Brachysema latifolium** and **Brachysema sericeum**.

Correa decumbens

Most correas have tubular to bell-shaped flowers which are pendent. In this species they are more commonly upright. They are narrow, red tipped with green, and are produced during spring and summer. Plants grow around 30cm to 1m tall, × 1–3m across. Regular light pruning from an early stage encourages dense, bushy growth.

Correa 'Dusky Bells'

Correa 'Dusky Bells' has bright pink, bell-shaped flowers of around 4cm long produced during autumn to spring. They are very much appreciated by native nectar-eating birds. Plants have a width of 2–3m, and are around 50cm tall. Regular light pruning promotes bushy growth.

Dampiera diversifolia

This very low growing plant has small green leaves and a showy display of bright, deep blue flowers of around 1cm across, seen mainly during spring to summer. It has a lightly suckering habit, and can cover an area of 1–2m across. Flowers best in a sunny situation. Excellent also as a container plant.

Dampiera linearis
Common Dampiera

There are many forms of this usually low-growing dampiera. Several grow to around 30cm tall, while some are taller. They spread by suckering lightly, and can cover an area of 1–2m across. During late winter to early summer they can provide an eye-catching display of small, deep blue flowers, which can literally cover the foliage.

Darwinia taxifolia ssp. macrolaena

This low, spreading shrub has a width of around 1–2m. The leaves are small, narrow and greyish green, providing a contrast to the showy clusters of bright pink to red flowers produced during spring and summer.

Goodenia hederacea
Forest Goodenia; Ivy Goodenia

A flat, groundcover species which can spread by lightly suckering to 1–2m across. It has yellow to orange flowers to 2cm across, produced in spring to summer or also into autumn. Other prostrate or low goodenias include **Goodenia elongata**, **G. geniculata**, **G. humilis** and **G. lanata**.

Grevillea

There are many prostrate *Grevillea* species which are excellent groundcover plants. Five species are described below, and others are included in the supplementary groundcover list.

Grevillea 'Bronze Rambler' has deeply divided leaves which often have reddish tonings and the deep red toothbrush flowers are produced mainly during spring to autumn. Plants can spread 3–5m across but are readily kept to 2m wide by pruning.

Grevillea × gaudichaudii. This is one of the most commonly cultivated groundcover grevilleas. It grows to around 30cm tall, and can spread 2–5m across. The leaves are attractively lobed, and the new foliage growth has burgundy tonings. Dark red toothbrush shaped flower-heads catch the attention of humans and nectar-eating birds during spring to autumn. Regular light pruning helps maintain vigour.

Grevillea juniperina, **prostrate forms**, Juniper Grevillea. There are several forms of this species, only some of which are prostrate. Others can grow to 4m tall. All have small, prickly pointed leaves, with a similarity to those of juniper plants. The prostrate forms can have buff, yellow or red flowers, produced mainly in winter and spring, and they can cover an area of 1–5m across. All respond well to pruning.

Grevillea laurifolia. This is another grevillea where the name makes reference to the foliage. In this case the dark green leaves have a similarity to laurel leaves, as used in the wreaths presented to athletes in early sporting competitions such as the Olympic Games. This prostrate species can spread to 2–4m across, and has dark red, toothbrush flower-heads, produced during spring and summer.

Grevillea 'Poorinda Royal Mantle'. This is a vigorous hybrid grevillea of prostrate habit with a spread of 3–4m. The leaves are usually lobed, and can be to 10cm long. Flowering is mainly during spring to autumn, when there is an attractive display of dark red, toothbrush flower-heads. Plants respond well to regular pruning, which encourages dense foliage growth and maintains vigour.

Grevillea thelemanniana, Spider-net Grevillea. There are several forms of this *Grevillea* species, including two attractive prostrate ones. A green-foliaged form has divided leaves with narrow segments and bright red flowers. It can spread to 2–3m across. A grey-foliaged form has a similar width, but is of more open habit. The foliage colour makes a very attractive contrast to its deep pinkish red flowers. Both forms usually flower from late autumn through to early summer.

Helichrysum apiculatum
Common Everlasting

This is a variable species, several forms of which are popular in cultivation. The foliage is silvery grey and clusters of small, bright yellow everlasting flowers provide a very showy display from spring through to early autumn. Forms which sucker readily should be cut back in late

Helichrysum bracteatum, 'Diamond Head'

autumn to about 5cm above ground level, to promote new growth and flowering for the coming season. They have a height of 30–60cm, and can spread by suckering to 1–2m across.

Helichrysum bracteatum 'Diamond Head'
Straw Flower

Helichrysum bracteatum is an extremely variable species. This particular selection is a small, perennial groundcover with a height of 20–30cm and a width to about 1m. Its delightful golden yellow everlasting daisies, of about 3cm diameter are seen mainly during spring and summer. Flowers best in a fairly sunny situation. Heavy frosts damage foliage.

Hemiandra pungens
Snake Bush

This prostrate plant may develop a fairly open habit, unless lightly pruned on a regular basis to encourage dense growth. It spreads to around 1–2m across. Flowering is during spring to autumn, when there can be a scattered or massed display. There are selections available with mauve-pink or white flowers. It flowers best in a sunny situation.

Hemiandra pungens

Hibbertia
Guinea flowers

There are around 140 species of *Hibbertia* in Australia, several of which are groundcovers or low shrubs, plus others which will trail across the ground, or climb if support is available. Some will spread by layering. Their main flowering period is during spring to autumn, and the small to large, open-petalled flowers are nearly all bright yellow. Groundcovers well worth growing for their floral display are the prostrate form of **Hibbertia obtusifolia**, **Hibbertia pedunculata**, **Hibbertia procumbens** and **Hibbertia vestita**.

Kennedia

Kennedia belongs to the pea family and contains a number of excellent groundcover plants plus other species which can be grown as groundcovers, but will climb up any other plants or other suitable supports.

Kennedia prostrata is known as Running Postman, because of its bright red pea flowers seen in spring to early summer. It can spread 1–3m across. A fairly similar, dark-leaved species is **Kennedia eximia**. **Kennedia carinata** is a more compact plant with dark pinkish red flowers. **Kennedia glabrata** can grow quickly to 1–2m across, and will bear a profuse display of brick-red, lightly fragrant flowers during spring. It can be short-lived, but is excellent as an initial, quick growing groundcover. Further species are listed in the Climbers section on page 40.

Kunzea pomifera
Muntries

This can grow as a fairly dense groundcover with small, crowded, oval leaves. Small white to cream flowers are produced in clusters during spring. The fruit is a small, edible, bluish berry. Plants may reach a height of 50cm, and can spread

Lasiopetalum macrophyllum

1–3m across. Excellent for sandy soils and embankments. Best suited to an open aspect. **Kunzea 'Badja carpet'** is somewhat similar but is not as compact.

Lasiopetalum macrophyllum

This *Lasiopetalum* is a variable species. One variant is a groundcover that is particularly useful for shaded areas, and growing beneath taller trees and shrubs. It can grow to 4m across. The leaves are somewhat oblong, to 10cm long. They are greyish green above with dense creamy and rusty hairs on the undersurface, and new growth has very attractive reddish or rusty tones. The clusters of small starry flowers produced during spring are cream and covered with rusty hairs.

Melaleuca violacea, prostrate form

Some forms of this species can grow 1–2m tall, but there is also a flat-topped, dwarf selection useful for groundcover purposes, which grows to around 1–2m across. The leaves are small and grey-green, and provide an attractive combination with the claw-like clusters of purple to violet flowers seen during spring. It is particularly useful for moist or wet situations.

Myoporum parvifolium
Creeping Myoporum

This is another somewhat variable species, but the form most commonly available is a groundcover of 10–30cm tall, spreading 1–3m across. It likes a fairly open situation and can provide good, dense foliage cover which is topped with small white, starry flowers during spring to autumn. Forms with purplish foliage and pale pink flowers are also grown.

Pratia pedunculata

Pratia pedunculata
Pratia

This is a very low-growing plant of carpeting habit, with small, oval leaves. It layers and suckers as it grows to cover small pockets of soil, such as between paving stones, or larger areas as available. It likes a moist but well-drained situation with some sunshine, and can be covered with profuse blue or white, starry flowers during spring to autumn.

Pultenaea pedunculata
Matted Bush-pea

If you have a well-drained, sunny or semi-shaded situation, this species can provide an attractive mat of small green leaves to 1–2m across, topped in spring with a profuse display of small pea-shaped flowers of orange or yellow with red. There are also selected cultivars, **Pultenaea pedunculata 'Pyalong Gold'**, which has all yellow flowers, and **Pultenaea pedunculata 'Pyalong Pink'** which has pink flowers. Plants usually spread by layering.

Pultenaea pedunculata

Scaevola
Fan-flowers

The common name given to this genus refers to the distinctive shape of the small, open-petalled flowers. There are several species of groundcover habit, some of which are just beginning to become more readily obtainable as an awareness of their beauty and usefulness increases. Some can flower almost throughout the year, and the main flower colours include white through pinks, mauves and bluish tones to rich purple.

Scaevola auriculata is a low, spreading plant of 1–3m across, and has deep blue-mauve and yellow flowers almost throughout the year.

Scaevola **'Mauve Clusters'** is a popular cultivar. It has a prostrate habit with a width of 1–2m. Its mauve flowers are seen mainly in spring to autumn.

Scaevola striata, Royal Robe grows to around 50cm tall × 1–2m across, with large, bluish purple flowers to around 2.5cm across. It flowers mainly in spring and summer. The selection **'Pink Perfection'** is a recent introduction.

Scaevola striata

Spyridium parvifolium
'Austraflora Nimbus'

This dense groundcover is a selection from a species which is more commonly an upright shrub. It spreads to around 1m across. Small white to cream flowers are produced in spring and summer, but the major decorative feature is the grey floral leaves which surround the flower clusters and are prominent for most of the year.

Viola hederacea
Native Violet

An excellent herbaceous groundcover for moist, shaded or semi-shaded situations. It has kidney-shaped leaves and spreads by layering. Plants can be fairly easily controlled, but under favourable conditions can spread 2m or more across. They can flower for most of the year, with the purple and white flowers being held on slender upright stems of around 10cm long.

A selection of additional groundcover plants

Acacia amblygona
   cultriformis 'Austraflora Cascade'
   pilosa
Asterolasia trymalioides
Astroloma humifusum
Baeckea ramosissima ssp. *prostrata*
Banksia blechnifolia
   petiolaris
   prostrata
   repens
Bauera rubioides prostrate forms
Bossiaea cordigera
   foliosa
   prostrata
Carpobrotus modestus
   rossii
Correa reflexa dwarf forms

Darwinia citriodora 'Austraflora
   Seaspray'
   glaucophylla
   grandiflora
   rhadinophylla
Dichondra repens
Disphyma crassifolium (syn. *D. australe*)
Eremophila glabra prostrate forms
Eutaxia microphylla
Frankenia pauciflora
Grevillea acanthifolia
   aquifolium prostrate forms
   confertifolia prostrate form
   depauperata prostrate form (syn.
     G. brownii)
   diffusa 'Holsworthy'
   diminuta
   lanigera prostrate form
   nudiflora
   repens
   synapheae
   thelemanniana ssp. *obtusifolia*
Helipterum anthemoides
Homoranthus flavescens
Isotoma fluviatilis

Kennedia microphylla
Kunzea 'Badja Carpet'
   muelleri
Lechenaultia formosa prostrate forms
Leptospermum rupestre
Mazus pumilio
Micromyrtus ciliata prostrate form
Montia australasica (syn. *Claytonia
   australasica*)
Myoporum debile
Oxylobium tricuspidatum
*Persoonia chamaepeuce
   chamaepitys*
Phyla nodiflora
Pimelea filiformis
Prostanthera saxicola var. *montana*
Ptilotus obovatus
Pultenaea polifolia var. *mucronata*
Rhagodia spinescens
Scaevola hookeri
   pallida
Scleranthus biflorus
Symphionema montanum
Wahlenbergia gloriosa
Xanthosia rotundifolia

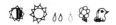
Conostylis candicans

Lilies and tufting plants

In many gardens there is often concentration on planting shrubs and trees, while clumping and tufting plants are neglected. This is such a pity!

The addition of plants with vertical or somewhat arching leaves of differing widths, provides variation in shape and texture which can make a garden more visually interesting, especially when they waft and wave in gentle winds. They are such a valuable group of plants, many of which can be simply stunning during their sometimes long flowering periods.

There is an increasing interest in native grasses, and although not in the spectacular flowering category, the intricacies of their minute flowers are fascinating underneath a magnifying glass.

So many of these plants will fit into quite small spaces, rarely can it be said that there is no room for extra tufting plants.

Anigozanthos
Kangaroo Paws

This is an extremely decorative group of plants, widely cultivated in gardens and for the cut-flower trade. The most vigorous and adaptable species is **Anigozanthos flavidus**, and many of the selected cultivars and hybrids now available have resulted from breeding programmes which involve this species. Some Kangaroo Paws are of dwarf habit, growing only to around 50cm tall by similar width, whilst others produce flower-stems of 2–3m tall, and foliage clumps to 2m across. The tubular flowers can be obtained in different shades and combinations of yellow, orange, pink, red and green. They grow best in a sunny situation, and most like moist but well-drained conditions.

Blandfordia grandiflora
Christmas Bells

A grass-like, tufting plant which can remain unnoticed in a garden until early summer, when the very showy, bell-shaped flowers of orange to red with yellow are produced on stems of 30–80cm tall. It grows best in a moist situation which receives sunshine for part of the day. It usually takes a few years until the first flowers are produced.

Blandfordia nobilis has smaller flowers.

Conostylis

This genus of around 30 species is closely related to *Anigozanthos*, the Kangaroo Paws. Most are low-growing plants, and form tufts or spreading clumps, usually with narrow, strap-like leaves. The main flower colour is yellow, and the tubular flowers which often have spreading lobes can be individual or clustered. Some species have cream to pinkish flowers. Their preference is generally for a sunny, well-drained situation. **Conostylis bealiana** develops as a tight clump, and is one of the most widely cultivated species. Its long, tubular flowers, which nectar-feeding birds find attractive, are produced during winter. Others such as **Conostylis aculeata** and **Conostylis candicans** have their main flowering in spring and early summer.

Craspedia globosa
Drumsticks

This species has silvery, strap-like leaves to 30cm long, forming a clump of about 40–80cm across. During spring and summer, and sometimes at other periods, yellow, dense globular flower-heads of around 2.5cm across are produced on upright stems to 1m tall. They are useful as fresh or dried cut-flowers.

Crinum pedunculatum
Swamp Lily; River Lily

A bulbous lily with leaves of 50cm–2m long × 10–15cm wide, forming a large, evergreen tussock. During spring to autumn loose heads of starry, fragrant white flowers are produced in clusters on stems to 80cm long. Sometimes plants may not flower every year.

Dianella
Flax Lilies

Around 15 *Dianella* species occur in Australia, with an almost equal number coming from Asia and the Pacific. **Dianella revoluta** and **Dianella tasmanica** are the most commonly cultivated, and are particularly useful for moist, shaded situations, although the former will also grow in a well-drained, sunny position. Both can form clumps to around 2m across. *D. tasmanica* is the taller of the two, with a height of around 60cm–1.7m. They have pale blue flowers on upright stems during spring to summer, followed by dark-blue, shiny berries, those of *D. tasmanica* are poisonous.

Diplarrena moraea
Butterfly Flag

This species forms a fairly open clump to around 60cm high by up to 1m across. The main flowering period is during late spring and summer, when three-petalled flowers are produced on upright stems. They are commonly white, white and yellow, or white with yellow and purple markings.

Glischrocaryon behrii
Golden Pennants

A clump-forming plant which can spread by suckering to produce colonies. The stems are leafless or with scattered, small leaves. During spring there is a profuse display of golden flower clusters. This species grows best in a well-drained, sunny situation. Plants are rejuvenated by pruning to ground level in late autumn.

Orthrosanthus
Morning Iris; Morning Flags

This is a genus of tufting plants with narrow, strap-like leaves. Clusters of beautiful pale to deep blue, open-petalled flowers are produced on upright stems during spring. The species most common in cultivation are **Orthrosanthus laxus**, **Orthrosanthus multiflorus** and **Orthrosanthus polystachyus**. They like a sunny situation, and will grow well in moist or well-drained positions.

Patersonia
Purple Flags

Patersonia is a widespread genus with several species worthy of a place in the garden. All are tufting or clump-forming with long, narrow leaves. The three-petalled flowers, which are commonly purple but may be yellow

Orthrosanthus polystachyus

or white, are produced on upright stems during spring to summer. Each flower lasts only one day, but is produced in succession over several weeks. In different species the stems may be shorter or longer than the leaves. They like similar conditions to *Orthrosanthus*. Species most commonly grown include **Patersonia fragilis** and **Patersonia occidentalis**.

Restio tetraphyllus
Tassel-cord Rush

In moist conditions, this clump-forming rush can grow 1–2m tall by a similar width. It has attractive foliage with narrow, spear-like, sometimes reddish, stems bearing plumes of soft, bright green foliage near the tips. During spring and summer tassels of reddish brown flowers and fruits add to its beauty.

Stylidium graminifolium
Grass Trigger-plant

This species has a small tuft of up to 30cm tall by similar width, with grass-like or strap-like leaves. During spring and summer, numerous pale to dark pink, small flowers are borne on upright stems to 1m or more in height. It is a widespread species, and the depth of flower colour and size of the stems can vary according to the area from which it has originated. Members of this genus are insect-pollinated, and during pollination the flower responds with a trigger-like action, depositing and collecting pollen from visiting insects. Other stylidiums, such

as the low, spreading **Stylidium bulbiferum** are also well worth growing.

Thelionema caespitosum
Tufted Lily

This species which until fairly recently was known as *Stypandra caespitosa*, forms a grass-like clump to 50cm high by a similar width, with bluish to grey-green leaves. During summer it produces a very attractive display of small, blue, starry flowers on slender, branched stems which are taller than the foliage. There is also a cream-flowered variant.

Thysanotus multiflorus
Fringe-lily

This is a very showy species, although not always easy to maintain in a garden over a long period. It has grass-like leaves forming a clump of around 50cm tall by similar width. During spring to early autumn it bears clusters of bright mauve flowers with fringed petals, which open during warm, sunny days. It should be grown in a warm, well-drained situation.

Xanthorrhoea species
Grass Trees

Xanthorrhoeas are tufting plants which are eagerly sought by many gardeners, but are very slow-growing from seed, and difficult to transplant or cultivate by other means. The development of seedlings is nevertheless well worth the wait for those who are patient. They form extremely attractive, grass-like tufts, which waft freely in the slightest of breezes. The trunks of most species develop very slowly. Upright flower stems with numerous small, very fragrant, creamy-white flowers, are produced during spring to summer, and these can be commonly seen in natural bushland areas. Plants do not flower regularly in gardens but if this occurs, it should be considered as a bonus.

Pterostylis nutans

Orchids

There are over 800 native orchid species within Australia. The majority of these are terrestrial plants, which grow in the ground, the rest are epiphytes, growing upon plants or rocks. Both groups have outstanding members which are very decorative. Some species have stringent cultivation requirements, whereas others do well even if virtually neglected. Slugs and snails are notorious for the damage they do to many terrestrials, especially the green-hoods, *Pterostylis* species.

Cymbidium madidum
Native Cymbidium

This epiphytic orchid forms large clumps and has leaves of 0.3–1m long. The highly fragrant flowers of around 2.5cm diameter are yellow-brown to green, and are produced in racemes of up to 70 flowers during late spring to summer. Grows well in containers and likes cool, humid conditions in a situation which has some air movement.

Dendrobium kingianum
Pink Rock Orchid

A very adaptable and widely grown orchid in bush-house, shadehouse or protected outdoor situations. It forms a clump of 0.2–0.5m in height. The flowers are commonly pink, 1–2cm diameter, and produced in spikes of up to 15 flowers during late winter to spring.

Dendrobium speciosum

Dendrobium speciosum
King Orchid; Rock Orchid

One of the easiest Australian orchids to cultivate either in a pot of orchid mix, or as an epiphyte on a log, stump or tree. It has thick, leathery leaves to 25cm long, and can form large clumps. White to deep yellow, fragrant flowers of 2–5cm diameter, are produced in racemes to 60cm long during spring. It grows best in a warm situation with protection from very hot sunshine and frosts. **Dendrobium falcorostrum** is somewhat similar, but with smaller leaves. The highly fragrant white to cream flowers are produced in shorter racemes.

Diuris
Donkey Orchids

Diuris are among the easiest to grow of the Australian terrestrial orchids. They are best grown in containers, in a shadehouse or protected situation with good ventilation. They are not well suited to a hot, humid glasshouse environment. The following are two recommended species.

Diuris longifolia has grass-like leaves to 20cm long. During spring upright stems to 30cm tall bear up to six purple and mauve flowers with yellow markings.

Diuris sulphurea has leaves to 50cm long with flower stems to 60cm tall. Its flowers are yellow with dark brown markings.

Pterostylis
Greenhoods, Maroonhoods and Rustyhoods

There are around 120 species of *Pterostylis* which can be fairly easily recognised by their hood-like floral structure. They are terrestrial orchids, many of which form colonies in nature, and these can be grown very successfully in containers. They grow well in a shadehouse or protected situation, and should be watered regularly while in active growth, but allowed to dry out when in their dormant period (usually during summer). Species most readily cultivated include **Pterostylis concinna**, **P. curta**, **P. nutans** and **P. pedunculata**, all of which flower during autumn or winter to spring.

Sarcochilus hartmannii

This orchid grows naturally on rocks and boulders, but adapts well to cultivation in containers. It has thick, fleshy leaves to 20cm long and during spring, glistening, white flowers, usually with crimson spots in the centre are produced in racemes of up to 25 blooms. Each flower is around 2–3cm across. It likes a warm, moist but well-drained, humid, situation with good light, but protection from extreme heat.

Adiantum aethiopicum

Adiantum
Maidenhair Ferns

🌓 ☀ 🌡 ◌◌ 🍃

There are many different maidenhair ferns, most of which occur outside Australia, but there are also some native species, which are widely grown. **Adiantum aethiopicum**, Common Maidenhair, has branched fronds and small rounded segments. It grows well in containers, provided it is not over-watered, or beneath other plants in gardens, where it receives filtered sunlight. Others worth considering include **Adiantum formosum** and **Adiantum hispidulum**.

Asplenium

🌓 ☀ 🌡 ◌◌ 🍃

This genus has around 26 Australian species, several of which are commonly cultivated. The best known are possibly **Asplenium australasicum** and **Asplenium nidus**, the Bird's Nest Ferns. Their fronds are not divided, as is most fern foliage, and they can be to 2m long × 20cm wide. They form large clumps and grow naturally in places such as the forks of large trees. In cultivation they can be grown in containers or garden situations. **Asplenium simplicifrons** has much smaller, undivided fronds, to 60cm × 3cm. **Asplenium bulbiferum**, Mother Spleenwort has divided, fern-like fronds to over 1m long, and forms a clump to 1.5m across. Young plantlets are frequently produced from the frond tips.

Ferns and fern allies

Ferns are distinguished from the majority of other garden plants in that they do not produce flowers. They reproduce from spores, which usually develop on the underside of the fronds or on separate fertile fronds.

Ferns are very popular garden plants, and their distinctive foliage provides year-round beauty. They are commonly regarded as shade-loving and moisture-loving plants, but many will grow well in quite open, well-drained situations.

Blechnum
Water Ferns

🌓 ☀ 🌡 ◌◌ 🍃

This group of ferns gains its common name from species frequently occurring in moist situations. Several are common in cultivation including **Blechnum fluviatile** and **B. pennamarina**, which are prostrate, spreading species. **Blechnum minus** — the soft water-fern, **Blechnum nudum** — the fishbone water-fern and **B. wattsii** — the hard water-fern each have fronds to around 1m long. All have a preference for a moist, sheltered situation.

Christella

🌓 ☀ 🌡 ◌◌ 🍃

There are around 60 ferns in this genus, but only five occur within Australia. **Christella dentata** has dark green, divided fronds and forms a clump to around 1m tall. It will grow well in a wide variety of garden situations.

Cyathea
Tree Ferns

🌓 ☀ 🌡 ◌◌ 🍃

Cyathea australis, the rough tree fern, is a very common fern in south-eastern Australia, which can be recognised by the rough texture at the base of each frond. It does not transplant as readily as *Dicksonia antarctica*, with which it is often confused. **Cyathea cooperi**, scaly tree fern can grow to 12m tall, but the trunk is usually no more than 15cm in diameter. This species occurs in Qld and NSW, and is one of the fastest growing Australian tree ferns.

Dicksonia antarctica
Soft Tree Fern

🌓 ☀ 🌡 ◌◌ 🍃

This species occurs on the east coast of Australia. It can grow to 15m tall with a thick trunk and fronds to over 4m long. The base of the fronds has a soft texture. This species does transplant readily, even if the trunk is cut above ground level. The fronds should be removed, and the base of the trunk buried to a depth of 20–25cm. Plants prefer a sheltered situation, and should be watered regularly during hot, dry periods.

Doodia
Rasp Ferns

🌓 ☀ ☼ 🌡 ◌◌ 🍃

A relatively small genus, with around six Australian species. **Doodia aspera**, prickly rasp fern, and **Doodia media**, common rasp fern, are fairly widely grown and are adaptable to a wide range of garden situations, including open sites where they receive some sunshine. Both grow to around 60cm tall × 1m across, and have decorative pink to purplish red new growth.

Doodia aspera

Marsilea
Nardoo

An unusual group of ferns with foliage resembling clover leaves. The spores are produced in a case formed by modified leaves and in some species these were made into a paste, a major part of the diet of Australian Aborigines. **Marsilea drummondii** and **M. mutica** are both fairly widely cultivated, and can be grown in or around ponds, or in other moist to waterlogged situations.

Platycerium
Elkhorns and Staghorns

These are well-known and distinctive epiphytic ferns. They are widely cultivated and commonly attached to timber slabs or logs. **Platycerium bifurcatum**, Elkhorn has fronds which are narrowly wedge-shaped near the base, branching into long, narrow segments near the tip, which is the area where spore is produced. Small plantlets develop near the base of the parent plant, and large clumps

can result. In **Platycerium superbum**, Staghorn, the spore is produced at the base of the pendulous, forked fronds. In this species new plantlets are not produced and the original plant grows larger each year. Both these species grow well in a sheltered situation where they are not allowed to dry out completely. Other species include the Northern Elkhorn, **Platycerium hillii** and the Silver Elkhorn, **Platycerium veitchii**.

Polystichum
Shield Ferns

Polystichum proliferum, Mother Shield Fern is the most commonly grown Australian species. It has fronds to 1m long × 30cm wide. It is common for new plantlets to form near the frond tips. In nature these develop into new plants as the fronds die and the plantlets come in contact with the soil. In cultivation they can be pegged down into pots, then cut from the parent plant as the new plants become established. This fern will tolerate some sunshine.

Marsilea mutica

Pteris
Brakes

This is a large genus of over 200 species, only a very small number of which occur within Australia. **Pteris tremula**, Tender Brake grows naturally in all states except Western Australia, in a wide range of situations. It develops into a large plant with multiple crowns with fronds to 2m long. **Pteris umbrosa**, Jungle Brake has fronds to around 1m with long, narrow segments. Both these species grow best in a moist, protected situation.

Shrubs

In other regions of the world, horticulturists often refer to Australia as the 'Great Shrubland'. There is a tremendous diversity in the shrubby flora of Australia, and there are literally hundreds of very desirable species from which the grower of Australian plants can choose.

The following charts list a selection of 120 species, suitable for cultivation in home gardens. Each one is of proven horticultural value and performance, and most are fairly readily obtainable, particularly from nurseries which specialise in Australian plants, see seed and plant suppliers on page 62.

Acacia
Wattle

We commonly think of wattles as being trees, but there are also numerous small to medium shrubs included within this very large genus with nearly 1000 different species.

Acacia drummondii ssp. **affinis** grows to around 1m tall, by similar width, and produces an excellent display of yellow rod-like flowers during winter and spring.

Acacia boormanii will grow to 3–5m tall, and can sucker lightly to form a copse. Its bright yellow flowers, in late winter to spring, can be extremely showy.

Acacia suaveolens, Sweet Wattle. This is a shrubby plant of 1–3m tall

with bluish green foliage. The pale yellow flower-heads are fragrant, and produced during autumn to spring.

Acacia vestita grows to 6m tall with a weeping habit and soft, hairy, greyish foliage. It flowers in late winter and spring with racemes of golden yellow flower-balls.

It is also worth checking out many of the other species, particularly if you are seeking a plant with yellow flowers as most wattles are very adaptable.

Alyogyne huegelii

A very close relative of *Hibiscus*, this evergreen species grows to around 2.5m tall. It is fairly quick-growing, and responds well to regular pruning, which is often required. It can form an upright shrub or can be trained almost horizontally along a fence or wall. It has whitish to deep mauve or purple flowers to 10cm across, which are produced throughout most of the year, but reach a peak during the warmest months.

Astartea fascicularis

This small-foliaged shrub grows 1–2.5m tall and can spread 2–3m across. Pink buds open to white or sometimes pink flowers from winter through to early autumn. Although the flowers are small, they provide a profuse and decorative display.

Astartea **'Winter Pink'** is a recently introduced cultivar with a profusion of small, pink flowers produced over a long period from winter through to summer. Plants grow to around 1.5m tall, respond well to pruning, and are grown commercially by the cut-flower trade.

Banksia
Banksia; Honeysuckles

This is a genus of outstanding ornamental value, but unfortunately many of the spectacular species from deep sandy regions of Western Australia will not tolerate the heavier soils and humidity which often exist in other areas. There are, however, some species from eastern Australia which are more adaptable in cultivation, including the following.

Banksia ericifolia grows 3–6m tall with small, somewhat heath-like leaves, and produces upright flower-spikes to 25cm long during autumn to spring. They can be in shades from golden yellow to orange or deep red.

Banksia spinulosa is similar, but often with serrated leaves to 8cm long. Its flower-spikes can be yellow or

Alyogyne huegelii

honey-coloured, with yellow, red or black styles. There are also excellent, low-growing forms of this species available.

Banksia marginata is a variable species with heights of 1–10m. It has smaller, yellow flower-spikes, to about 10cm long, produced from autumn to spring.

Banksia robur differs from those above in being able to tolerate moist to wet conditions. It grows around 1–3m tall, with the main decorative feature being the flower-buds which are a rich bluish green. These open to yellow-green flowers in broad spikes of up to 15cm long, produced sporadically throughout the year.

Bauera rubioides
Wiry Bauera

This is a variable shrub of around 30cm–3m tall. It can flower almost throughout the year. With white to pink open-petalled flowers to 2cm across. It adapts to a wide range of situations, including shade to full sun, and will also cope with moist to wet conditions. It grows well in informal combination with other plants.

Boronia
Boronia

This is a genus of almost 100 Australian species, well known because of two or three which are very spectacular in flower or fragrance.

A selection of shrubs to around 1 metre tall

Plant names asterisked are discussed in detail in the text.

Acacia drummondii ssp. *affinis* var. *parviflora*
Baeckea ramosissima
Beaufortia schaueri
Boronia serrulata
Correa reflexa
Cryptandra amara
Darwinia lejostyla
Dodonaea microzyga
Epacris pulchella
  reclinata
Eremophila glabra
Grevillea curviloba
  lavandulacea
Halgania cyanea
Homoranthus papillatus
Lechenaultia biloba
  formosa
Melaleuca thymifolia
Micromyrtus ciliata
Olearia teretifolia compact form
Pimelea ferruginea
Prostanthera aspalathoides
Rhododendron lochae
Tetratheca thymifolia
Thomasia grandiflora
  pygmaea
Xanthosia rotundifolia

Banksia ericifolia

There also are others which are highly desirable, but not widely grown.

Boronia megastigma is the well known Brown Boronia highly prized for the fragrance of its reddish brown, brown or lime green pendent, cupped flowers produced in spring. It grows best if regularly pruned to 1m or less in height. Plants like a protected situation and the root system should not be allowed to dry out.

Boronia heterophylla and **B. molloyae** both have deep pinkish red flowers which last for a long time on the plant, or when used as cut-flowers. Both grow around 1–3m tall and respond well to pruning.

Boronia muelleri

Boronia muelleri is a variable species with forms from 50cm to around 6m in height. It has ferny foliage and lightly fragrant, open-petalled, pink flowers which can be borne in profusion during spring, with scattered blooms at other times. The selection **B. muelleri 'Sunset Serenade'** is particularly floriferous.

Boronia pinnata grows 1–2m tall and is another species with pink, open-petalled flowers seen mainly in spring to early summer. The ferny foliage has a camphor-like fragrance. This is a species which will tolerate a fair amount of sunshine and responds very well to pruning.

Callistemon
Bottlebrushes

Callistemons are well-known for their showy flower-spikes, and often extended flowering seasons. They are also well-known to honey-eating birds which delight in their abundant supply of nectar. Most are very adaptable in cultivation, and will grow well in moist or well-drained situations. The main flowering period is during spring to early summer, but some species can also flower in autumn if they have

received summer moisture. Under favourable conditions they will bloom throughout the year. They flower best in sunny positions.

The most popular species over the years have been those with bright red flower-spikes including **Callistemon citrinus**, which grows 2–8m tall, **Callistemon viminalis** a variable and often weeping plant, growing from a low shrub to a tree of 10–12m tall, and the cultivar **Callistemon 'Harkness'**, with its bright red bottlebrushes to 15cm long.

Callistemon pallidus is an attractive shrub of 2–5m tall with cream to yellow brushes. It has silvery to reddish new foliage growth which is a decorative feature of several species. There is also a low growing selection, 'Australflora Candle Glow'.

Other species and cultivars which are becoming popular have flower colours of white, pale to deep pink, mauve to violet, and deep reds to burgundy.

Callistemon citrinus

Calothamnus quadrifidus
Common Net-bush

This is a very adaptable garden plant able to tolerate moist to quite dry situations, but it may suffer damage from heavy frosts. It flowers best in a fairly sunny site. Leaves are narrow and green to greyish green and bright red claw-like flowers are produced in spikes to about 30cm long on the older wood, during spring to autumn. Grows 2–4m × 2–5m, but responds well to pruning.

Calytrix tetragona
Common Fringe-myrtle

Members of the genus *Calytrix* are mostly small to medium shrubs with small, often aromatic leaves and open-petalled, starry flowers. *Calytrix tetragona* grows 1–2m tall by a similar width, and benefits from pruning. Selections with white, pale pink or deep pink flowers, produced during spring, are available.

Cassia artemisioides
Silver Cassia

Cassias are renowned for their usually bright yellow, bell-shaped or cupped flowers, and for their ability to withstand long periods of dryness. This species grows 1–2m tall by a similar width, and has silvery, divided leaves. Delicately fragrant flowers can be produced throughout most of the year. Responds well to pruning.

Chamelaucium uncinatum
Geraldton Wax

This species is grown extensively by the cut-flower trade. It is a shrub of 2–5m tall which can be of open habit, but regular pruning will encourage bushy growth. During spring to early summer there is a showy display of white, pink, or mauve to reddish purple flowers of about 2.5cm across. Several named cultivars are available. Grows best in a sunny, well-drained situation.

Calothamnus quadrifidus

In this garden you gain a vista with *Grevillea speciosa* in the foreground and your eyes are led to *Acacia plicata* with its soft, ferny foliage and golden yellow flower-heads. In the background the brilliance of the hybrid waratah *Telopea oreades* × *speciosissima* stands out like a series of beacons. Design and planting Kath Deery.

A semi-wilderness in a small suburban front garden where tree ferns, ground ferns and other shade-loving plants thrive beneath the canopy of various eucalypts and silver birches. Design and construction Rodger Elliot and John Bird.

ABOVE The brilliance of the sometimes wayward *Epacris longiflora*, fuchsia heath, is evident even on an overcast day. Being able to see past pleasing tree trunks such as this *Eucalyptus leucoxylon* subspecies *megalocarpa* can create an illusion of greater space in a small area. *Cyathea australis*, hard tree fern, has been used for screening purposes. Design and construction Diana and Brian Snape.

BELOW A semi-shaded reflective pool is enhanced by moisture and shade-loving plants of differing forms and textures and is an ideal place for relaxing. *Restio tetraphyllus*, ferns and water plants such as *Marsilea*, nardoo, as well as soft-foliaged native grasses are complimentary to the pool and its surrounds. Design and construction Kevin Hoffman.

ABOVE A heathland-like effect is gained with dense planting of groundcovers such as *Grevillea laurifolia* and *Brachyscome multifida* 'Breakoday' informally interspersed with small, colourful flowering shrubs. The density of foliage helps to reduce weed infestation and compaction of the soil by rainfall or supplementary watering.

BELOW In Tresco Abbey Gardens on the Scilly Isles off the coast of Cornwall, England, this handsome, aged and well-pruned *Bursaria spinosa* is growing amongst plants from various parts of the world.

ABOVE A low, gently sloping embankment with shrubby Californian *Diplacus* hybrids in the foreground. In the background there is *Cassinia aculeata* (cream), *Prostanthera* 'Poorinda Bride' (pale mauve) and *Helichrysum bracteatum* 'Dargan Hill Monarch' (yellow).

BELOW A suburban house with *Eucalyptus citriodora* providing summer shade but allowing excellent penetration of winter sun. The quick growing and vigorous *Kennedia nigricans* needs strong supports on which to climb and develop a dense cover of foliage. It is not recommended for wooden fences because of its vigour. Design and construction Paul Thompson.

A selection of shrubs generally around 1–2 metres tall

Plant names asterisked are discussed in detail in the text.

*Astartea fascicularis
   *'Winter Pink'
*Asterolasia asteriscophora
*Bauera rubioides
Beaufortia purpurea
*Boronia heterophylla
   *megastigma
   *molloyae
   *muelleri
   *pinnata
Brachysema celsianum
*Calytrix tetragona
*Cassia artemisioides
Chorizema cordatum
*Correa alba
   *baeuerlenii
   *glabra
   *'Mannii'
   *pulchella
   *reflexa
*Crowea exalata
*Darwinia citriodora
*Epacris impressa
   *longiflora
Eriostemon australasius
   *myoporoides
   verrucosus
*Grevillea alpina
   *lavandulacea
   *'Mason's Hybrid'
   *'Robyn Gordon'
   *sericea
   *speciosa ssp. dimorpha
*Guichenotia macrantha
*Helichrysum bracteatum
*Homoranthus darwinioides
*Hypocalymma angustifolium
Isopogon anemonifolius
*Leptospermum macrocarpum
Melaleuca violacea
*Olearia phlogopappa
   *teretifolia
*Phebalium lamprophyllum
Prostanthera incana
   stricta
Regelia ciliata
*Templetonia retusa
*Thryptomene calycina
   *saxicola
Westringia glabra

Correa reflexa

Correa
Correa

There are around 11 different correas all native to Australia, plus numerous cultivar selections and hybrids. Most are small, shrubby plants, and all are suitable for garden cultivation. Their flowers are commonly bell-shaped, pendent, and 2–4cm long. They can be cream, green, pink to red, or in various combinations of these colours. Most are very attractive to nectar-feeding birds.

Correa alba is an exception to the above, in that the flowers are white, and the tube splits to form an almost open-petalled, starry flower. It is a shrub of up to 2m tall which grows naturally in coastal situations, and is therefore ideal for use in gardens with these conditions. Tolerates hard pruning or clipping.

Correa baeuerlenii grows 1–2m tall and has green flowers with a flattened calyx, giving it the common name of Chef's Cap Correa, while **Correa glabra** is another bushy species usually with green flowers. Both are excellent screening or hedging plants.

Recommended correas with pink to red, bell-shaped flowers include **Correa 'Mannii'** which grows 1–2.5m tall and **Correa pulchella** which grows up to 1.5m tall.

Correa reflexa is an extremely variable species, with forms which are prostrate or up to 3m tall. The flowers are commonly red tipped with green, cream or yellow, and can be produced from autumn through to spring. There are also forms with cream or green flowers.

All species respond well to pruning.

Crowea exalata
Small Crowea

This is a variable, and very attractive species, the most commonly cultivated form being a shrub of around 1–1.5m tall. It has small, aromatic leaves and pink, starry flowers to 2cm across, produced mainly in spring to autumn. There are two other *Crowea* species, plus a small number of hybrids and cultivars, all of which are well worth growing. All are excellent, long-lasting cut-flowers.

Cryptandra amara
Bitter Cryptandra

This is a small shrub of around 30cm to 1m in height, with stiff branchlets and small green leaves. It is fairly inconspicuous until late autumn to spring, when the foliage can become completely covered with an abundance of very small, white, tubular flowers. It prefers a semi-shaded situation, and during the flowering period, will certainly brighten up any dull areas of the garden. Responds very well to pruning.

Darwinia citriodora
Lemon-scented Myrtle

The genus *Darwinia* with around 60 different species occurs only in Australia. Many are extremely showy, but some of these have proved difficult to maintain in cultivation. *Darwinia citriodora* is more adaptable, and has been used as a rootstock for the grafting of some of the other more troublesome members of the genus. It is a shrub of 50cm–2m tall with attractive, greyish green, aromatic foliage. The flower-clusters are orange to red with green, and are produced mainly during winter to early summer. Plants respond well to regular light pruning.

Dryandra formosa
Showy Dryandra

There are over 50 different *Dryandra* species, all of which are found in south-western WA. *Dryandra formosa* is one of the showiest and easiest to cultivate, provided it is grown in well-drained soils, with partial or full sun. It is usually a shrub of 3–4m tall, but can become taller in very favourable situations. The foliage is decorative, with narrow, softly toothed leaves to 20cm long. Rich yellow-orange flower-heads to 10cm across are produced at the branchlet tips during winter to late spring. They are excellent for use as cut-flowers, either fresh or dried.

Epacris longiflora
Fuchsia Heath

This is an eye-catching plant with pendent, tubular flowers of red tipped with white, which can be produced throughout the year. It has an open growth habit with a height of 50cm–1m, and similar width. It does have the potential to grow larger, but such specimens can decrease in vigour and attractiveness. This can be corrected by light pruning at least once per year.

Many other *Epacris* species or Native Heaths are also worthy of cultivation, including the following, which all grow to around 1m tall. All respond well to pruning, which encourages bushy growth. **Epacris impressa**, Common Heath, has white or pink to red, tubular flowers to 2cm long during autumn to spring. The short, tubular flowers of **Epacris pulchella**, Coral Heath, are usually pink, while those of **Epacris reclinata** are commonly reddish pink.

Eremophila glabra
Common Emu-bush

The name *Eremophila* means 'desert-loving', and this is an apt description for many species. *Eremophila glabra* is one which will adapt to a range of

Epacris longiflora

soils, and there are several different forms with heights ranging from 20cm to around 1.5m. The flowers are tubular, in shades of yellow to red or green, and are produced mainly during winter to early autumn. Grows best in a sunny situation.

Eriostemon myoporoides
Long-leaved Waxflower

This is a densely foliaged shrub of 1–2m tall with aromatic leaves. During winter to early summer white, starry flowers of 2–5cm across open from pale to deep pink buds. It will grow and flower well in sun or semi-shade. An excellent cut-flower.

Goodia lotifolia
Golden Tip

Clover Tree is another common name for this shrubby species, because the leaves are produced in threes. It belongs to the pea family, and has a showy display of lightly fragrant, yellow with red flowers during autumn to late spring. Plants can grow 1–5m tall, but respond well to pruning. Has a preference for semi-shaded situations.

Grevillea
Grevillea

This is a genus of outstanding horticultural importance, with around 250 species and numerous cultivars, the majority of which are shrubby plants. A selection of those which have proved highly desirable in cultivation is listed below, and for a wider range of species readers are referred to other publications as listed in the Further Reading section.

Grevillea alpina is an extremely variable species. There are many different forms of growth habit, with plants ranging from 20cm–2.5m tall. Flower colour is another variable feature, and these include combinations of white, cream, yellow, orange, pink and red.

Grevillea curviloba can be grown as a prostrate shrub to 0.5m tall × 2–4m across, if upright stems are removed after flowering. It has small, light green leaves and masses of sweetly scented, cream flowers, produced during spring. Responds very well to pruning.

Grevillea lavandulacea is known as the Lavender Grevillea because of the small, greyish leaves with an appearance similar to those of Lavender. They provide an excellent contrast to the bright pink to red flowers produced during winter and spring. This is another variable species, and there are several forms available with heights ranging from 0.5m–2.5m.

Grevillea longistyla hybrid is a large, bushy shrub of 2–5m tall by 2–4m across. It has reddish stems and divided, dark green leaves with narrow segments. Glossy pink to red flowers are produced in clusters during winter and spring. Responds well to pruning.

Grevillea 'Pink Surprise'. This is a cultivar of fairly recent origin. It is a large shrub of 3–5m tall with grey-green, divided leaves and large spikes of pink and cream flowers, produced beyond the foliage, throughout most of the year. It likes a sunny situation, with good drainage.

Grevillea 'Poorinda Constance' is an excellent bird-attracting cultivar which produces clusters of bright red flowers throughout most of the year, with a peak in winter to early spring. It is a large shrub growing around

A selection of shrubs growing taller than 2 metres

Plant names asterisked are discussed in detail in the text.

* *Acacia boormanii*
  * *suaveolens*
  * *vestita*
* *Alyogyne huegelii*
* *Banksia ericifolia*
  * *marginata*
  * *robur*
  * *spinulosa*
* *Callistemon citrinus*
  * *'Harkness'*
  * *pallidus*
  * *viminalis*
* *Calothamnus quadrifidus*
* *Chamelaucium uncinatum*
  Dodonaea sinuolata ssp. *acrodentata*
* *Dryandra formosa*
* *Goodia lotifolia*
* *Grevillea longistyla* hybrid
  * *'Pink Surprise'*
  * *'Poorinda Constance'*
  * *'Poorinda Queen'*
  * *speciosa* ssp. *speciosa*
  * *victoriae*
* *Hakea francisiana*
  * *laurina*
  Hibiscus heterophyllus
  Jacksonia scoparia
* *Kunzea baxteri*
  Lambertia formosa
* *Leptospermum petersonii*
  * *rotundifolium*
* *Melaleuca decussata*
  * *diosmifolia*
  * *fulgens*
  * *hypericifolia*
  * *incana*
  * *nesophila*
* *Persoonia pinifolia*
* *Prostanthera ovalifolia*
  * *rotundifolia*
* *Telopea speciosissima*
* *Westringia fruticosa*

Hakea sericea

1.5–3m tall by a similar width. Responds very well to pruning.

Grevillea 'Poorinda Queen' is extremely similar to *G.* 'Poorinda Constance', except that the flowers are a pale orange to apricot colour.

Grevillea 'Robyn Gordon' is one of the most popular grevilleas in cultivation at the present time. It is a shrub of 1–2m tall, with large clusters of bright red flowers, produced throughout most of the year.

Grevillea 'Mason's Hybrid' (also known as *Grevillea* 'Ned Kelly') is very similar, but the flowers are an orange-red.

Grevillea sericea is another grevillea which will flower throughout the year. Several forms are obtainable, and flower colours include white, pink and deep mauve-pink. Plants grow to around 2.5m tall by a similar width. Does not attract nectar-feeding birds.

Grevillea speciosa. There are several different forms of this species which are popular in cultivation. **Grevillea speciosa ssp. dimorpha** grows 1–2m tall, with broad or narrow leaves, and has clusters of brilliant red flowers during autumn to spring. **Grevillea speciosa ssp. speciosa** also has red flowers, but in wheel-like formation, giving it the common name of Red Spider-flower. It grows 1.5–3m tall with an upright or spreading habit, and can be successfully pruned to a desired form.

Grevillea thelemanniana is an extremely variable, and highly desirable grevillea. There are already selections included in the groundcover section. Within the shrubby variants there are many excellent, highly ornamental plants from which to choose. They can have green to greyish foliage and the tight clusters of flowers vary from pinks to reds.

Grevillea victoriae is also variable, and perhaps the best selections to grow are those from Mt. Wellington, Vic. (also sold as *G. miqueliana*), and one from East Gippsland, Vic. The former grows to 2.5m × 3m and has somewhat oval leaves and pendent clusters of lax, orange-red flowers, while the latter develops to 2–3m × 3–4m and has narrow leaves and pendent, spreading flower-heads. Both flower during winter and spring and respond well to pruning.

Guichenotia macrantha

A particularly beautiful plant with a sometimes confusing name. It is pronounced Gee-shen-o-tee-a. It is a shrub of 1–1.5m tall with grey-green foliage. During winter and spring it provides a showy display of pendent, lantern-shaped, pinkish mauve flowers to 1.5cm long. They have a papery texture, and are long lasting both on the plant, and after picking. Likes a fairly open, well-drained situation. Pruning helps overcome legginess.

Hakea

This genus is closely related to *Grevillea*, but is usually distinguished by the woody fruits which are retained on the plants for a long period. Several species are commonly cultivated, the majority of which are large shrubs to small trees.

Hakea francisiana grows 2.5–8m tall and has long, narrow, silvery-green leaves. During winter and spring it has a very showy display of rich pink to red flower-spikes to 10cm long. Likes a sunny situation and must have well-drained soils. Does best in low rainfall regions. Grafted plants which cope well in heavy soils are sometimes available.

Hakea laurina, Pincushion Hakea, is a plant of around 3–8m tall. Its red and cream flowers are produced in pincushion-like balls during autumn to spring. The buds can be damaged by heavy frost. Grows best in a position with good drainage.

Some species such as **Hakea sericea** have very prickly foliage, and are excellent refuge plants for native birds. During winter it produces a massed display of white or pink flowers. **Hakea salicifolia** is another widely grown species, and is useful for windbreak and screen planting. It does however have the potential to spread by seeding and could become an unwanted weed. It is not recommended for planting if there are areas of bushland nearby. This species is used as the grafting stock for *Hakea francisiana*.

Helichrysum
Everlastings; Straw Flowers

Plants in this genus have become popular because of their beauty in the garden, and their use both as cut-fresh and dried flowers.

Helichrysum bracteatum is a variable species with annual and perennial forms. Their height varies from around 30cm–1.5m. Most have bright golden yellow, everlasting daisy flower-heads produced over a long period, with a peak in spring to autumn. Flower colours can also include white, cream and pink. The plants are generally quick-growing, and respond well to an application of slow-release fertiliser applied in spring. They like a sunny situation with moist, but well-drained soils.

Helichrysum bracteatum 'Dargan Hill Monarch' is a perennial selection which grows as a shrub to around 1m tall, with large flower-heads of 6–8cm across. Regular pruning is beneficial.

Homoranthus

This is an Australian genus of seven species belonging to the Myrtle family.

Homoranthus darwinioides has been cultivated for many years, and grows as a fairly open shrub, to 1.5m tall. It has very small, greyish leaves, and small, cream to reddish, tubular flowers which hang in pairs from the branchlets, and are produced throughout most of the year. Attractive to nectar-feeding birds.

Homoranthus papillatus has the disparaging common name of mouse plant, or mouse and honey plant, resulting from the floral fragrance. It grows 50cm–1m × 1–2m with attractive, horizontal branches and small, greyish leaves, and is worth growing for these features alone. During spring to summer it produces small, yellow, somewhat honey-scented flowers. The fragrance can be quite strong, and it is recommended that it not be planted too close to doors or windows.

Hypocalymma angustifolium
White Myrtle

This is a shrub of 1–1.5m tall, and the commonly grown selections provide a delightful combination of pink and white during winter to spring. The small, clustered flowers are initially white, then deepen to dark pink as they mature. The foliage is somewhat open, with small, narrow leaves. Grows well in combination with other plants, in a situation with full or filtered sunshine. It is an excellent cut-flower and plants respond well to pruning.

Kunzea baxteri

Kunzea belongs to the Myrtle family, and there are several species grown in Australian gardens. **Kunzea baxteri** is a shrub of around 2–4m tall, by a similar width. During late autumn to spring it has outstanding, bright red flower-spikes, tipped with gold, very similar in general appearance to the bottlebrush spikes of Callistemons. It can be slow to flower initially, and seems to flower best if grown in harsh, well-drained to dry situations. Plants propagated from cuttings will often flower at an earlier age than those grown from seed.

Lechenaultia

This is a genus of small, shrubby plants which occur mainly in south-western WA. They have very decorative flowers, but some have proved difficult in cultivation. Their general preference is for well-drained, sandy soils, and an uncrowded, sunny situation. The following are the species most commonly grown in gardens. They can also be grown successfully as container plants. Lechenaultias are sometimes not long-lived in cultivation, but they can be propagated readily from cuttings to ensure a regular supply for your garden. **Lechenaultia biloba**, Blue

Lechenaultia, can grow 50cm–1m tall with very showy flowers, ranging from light to deep blue, or occasionally, white. These are produced at the branchlet tips during winter to early summer.

Lechenaultia formosa is a variable and floriferous species, with some prostrate forms and others to around 60cm tall. It can flower from autumn through to late spring, and there are several colour forms including vivid shades of yellow, orange, pink, bright red, and deep red.

Lechenaultia biloba

Leptospermum
Tea-trees

Within Australia there are 70 different tea-trees, most of which produce a floriferous display of white flowers during spring. Leptospermums have tended to lose favour over the years, because they have gained the reputation of being prone to scale attack, and the blackening of stems with sooty mould. This condition is particularly prevalent in many of the exotic hybrids. Australian tea-trees however, are less prone to these problems and there are a number of outstanding selections available.

Leptospermum macrocarpum is an attractive and adaptable species. Two selections, better known as *Leptospermum lanigerum* var. *macrocarpum* and *Leptospermum nitidum* 'Copper Sheen', and likely to be seen in nurseries under these names, are commonly grown. The former grows to about 1.5–2.5m high by a similar width, and has lovely reddish, new growth. The large, open flowers have pinkish petals. The latter is usually a compact shrub of 1–2.5m × 2–3m, and the older leaves have a coppery or bronzish toning, while the new growth is reddish. Its flowers have yellowish petals.

Leptospermum petersonii, Lemon-scented Tea-tree, is grown primarily for the beauty and fragrance of its foliage, rather than for the white to cream flowers, seen mainly during summer. It can grow 2–5m tall, × 2–3m across with soft, narrow, lemon-scented leaves of around 2–5cm long. New leaves have pink to bronze tonings. Plants respond well to pruning, which promotes new growth.

Leptospermum rotundifolium, Round-leaf Tea-tree. (Previously known as *Leptospermum scoparium* var. *rotundifolium*.) This species is known primarily by a number of attractive selections which flower during late spring. The 'Jervis Bay' variant usually has an upright growth habit, to 2–2.5m tall, and has bluish mauve flowers to 3cm across. 'Lavender Queen' is a spreading shrub of about 1.5m × 2m, and has large, pale mauve-pink flowers.

Leptospermum macrocarpum

Melaleuca
Honey-myrtles; Paperbarks

Melaleuca is a genus of over 150 species ranging from low, spreading groundcovers to tall trees. The flowers have small petals, but conspicuous stamens which are grouped together in five bundles. They are usually arranged in bottlebrush-like spikes, or

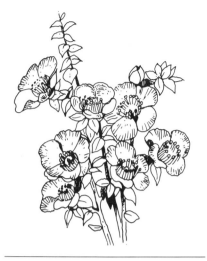

Leptospermum rotundifolium

globular heads. Several species have decorative trunks, including some with layers of papery bark, giving rise to the common name of Paperbarks. Melaleucas come from a wide range of soil and climatic conditions, but many of the species commonly available through nurseries will grow well in either moist or well-drained situations. They flower best in a sunny position.

Melaleuca decussata, Totem Poles. This is a dense shrub of 2–4m tall by a similar width, with small, greyish leaves. Some forms have a weeping habit. Pale to deep mauve flowers in bottlebrushes of 2–3cm long are produced during spring and summer.

Melaleuca diosmifolia has unusual, green bottlebrush flower-spikes produced during spring to early summer. It grows as a dense shrub of 2–4m tall by a similar width, and has decorative foliage, with small leaves crowded along the branchlets. It flowers best in harsh, well-drained situations, but grows vigorously and is often slow to flower in situations where there is a good supply of moisture and nutrients. Excellent for attracting nectar-feeding birds. Heavy frosts usually damage plants.

Melaleuca fulgens, Scarlet Honey-myrtle grows 1.5–3m tall and is a somewhat open shrub with grey-green foliage. The flowering period is during spring to early summer, and various forms of this species are available with flower colours of red, deep pink or salmon pink. A very showy plant when in full bloom.

Melaleuca hypericifolia is a dense shrub which flowers well and provides a good supply of nectar for

the native birds during summer. It grows 3–6m tall with a slightly weeping habit, but can be pruned to a smaller size if desired. The orange-red flowers are in spikes to 8cm long. This species can become a weed in some areas, and is therefore not recommended for planting near bush areas in regions beyond its natural habitat in NSW.

Melaleuca incana grows 2–3m tall by a similar width, and is popular mainly for the beauty of its pendulous, greyish foliage. The flowers are pale yellow, and produced in brushes to 5cm long during spring to early summer. The very compact, dwarf cultivar, 'Velvet Cushion' must have a sunny, open site, as it is prone to grey mould attack.

Melaleuca nesophila is another large, summer-flowering species. It grows 3–6m tall, and with some pruning can be encouraged to be bushy to ground level, or it can be grown on a trunk. The flowers are in globular heads of 2–3cm across, and are mauve-pink tipped with gold.

Melaleuca thymifolia grows only 50cm–1.5m tall. It has grey-green leaves which combine attractively with the mauve to purple flowers or rarely white, produced from spring to autumn. It likes a sunny situation, and will tolerate well-drained, moist or seasonally wet conditions.

Micromyrtus ciliata

Micromyrtus ciliata
Fringed Heath-myrtle

This species has prostrate forms, as well as shrubby forms to around 1m tall. The leaves are small and aromatic. During autumn to spring there is a showy display of small, white flowers, which deepen in colour to red as they mature, providing an attractive combination of white and pink to red.

Olearia
Daisy-bushes

Many members of the Daisy family are herbaceous annuals or perennials, however Olearias are small to large, woody shrubs with soft-petalled, white, pink, mauve, purple or blue daisy flowers. They generally flower best in a situation which receives partial to full sun.

Olearia phlogopappa, Dusty Daisy-bush grows 1.5–2.5m tall and several different forms are available, with flower colours covering the full range mentioned above. Main flowering period is during late winter and spring. Regular light pruning is recommended for this species.

Olearia teretifolia, Cypress Daisy-bush is a shrub which provides a profuse display of small, white daisy flowers during spring. It is normally a somewhat open shrub of around 1–2m tall by similar width, but there is also a compact form which has dense, conifer-like foliage, and usually reaches less than 1m tall.

Olearia phlogopappa

Persoonia pinifolia
Pine-leaved Geebung

As the name suggests, this is a plant with narrow, pine-like leaves. It grows 2–5m tall with small yellow flowers in spikes, which develop progressively from mid-summer through to winter. These are followed by clusters of green to purplish fruits, which formed part of the diet of Aborigines.

Phebalium lamprophyllum
Shiny Phebalium

A bushy shrub of 1–2m tall by similar width with dark green leaves, and white to cream flowers produced in clusters at the ends of the branchlets, during late winter to early summer. It is excellent for shady dry sites. Also in the same genus, **Phebalium squamulosum** is a variable shrub with showy, cream to bright yellow flower-heads, produced in spring to summer.

Pimelea ferruginea

This is a rounded shrub of around 50cm–1.5cm tall with small, shiny leaves. The flowers are pink to reddish, and produced in semi-globular heads at the tips of the branchlets, during winter and spring. **Pimelea ferruginea 'Bon Petite'** is a selection which has deep pink flowers, while **'Magenta Mist'** has magenta with white flowers. Butterflies find the flowers very attractive. Regular light pruning is recommended to maintain bushy growth and increase flower production.

Prostanthera
Mint-bushes

The Australian Mint-bushes are renowned for the fragrance of their foliage, as well as for the showy display of mauve, purple, pink or white flowers, produced by many species. They come from a wide range of natural habitats, but generally prefer a semi-shaded situation, in soils which remain slightly moist for most of the year.

Prostanthera aspalathoides is a notable exception to the above, as it likes a sunny, warm to hot, well-drained situation. It is a shrub of around 0.5m tall, and can spread to 1m across. Its flowering season is during late winter to summer, and the

Pimelea ferruginea 'Bon Petite'

flower colours of yellow, orange, pink or red are also different from those of most other Prostantheras.

Prostanthera ovalifolia, Mint-bush. This is the most commonly cultivated species, and it certainly provides an eye-catching display of usually purple flowers, which can cover the foliage during spring or early summer. Plants grow to around 2–4m tall with oval, toothed leaves. They respond well to pruning after flowering.

Postanthera rotundifolia, Round-leaf Mint-bush grows 1.5–2.5m tall with rounded, aromatic leaves. The flowering period is during spring, and both purple and pink flowered forms are commonly grown. Pruning after flowering is recommended.

Prostanthera rotundifolia

Rhododendron lochae

This is currently the only Australian rhododendron species, and it grows as a shrubby epiphytic plant in its natural rainforest habitat in Queensland. In cultivation it is usually a small shrub of 1–1.5m tall with shiny, oval leaves and waxy, red bell-shaped flowers to 5cm long, produced mainly in late summer and autumn. Likes a warm, sheltered situation with moist but well-drained soil. A number of selected forms are grown.

Telopea speciosissima
NSW Waratah

This species is the floral emblem of New South Wales, and is very well known for its spectacular, large red flower-heads, produced during spring. Some gardeners grow these plants

Telopea speciosissima

with great ease, while others have difficulty. It likes organically rich soil which is moist but well-drained, and a cool root area. Sunshine on the upper parts of the plant will help encourage good flowering. Plants can grow with fairly upright habit to 3–5m tall. They respond well to pruning after flowering, or cutting of the flower-stems. White-flowered forms and other particular selections, as well as hybrids, are also obtainable.

Templetonia retusa
Cockies Tongues

This is usually an upright shrub of 1.5–2.5m tall. The wedge-shaped leaves are greyish green, and during winter to spring there is a showy display of large, pink to red pea-flowers. There is also a white-flowered form, but this is rare in cultivation. Excellent for alkaline soils.

Tetratheca
Black-eyed Susan

Common names can sometimes be confusing, and this is one good example, as there are other non-Australian plants also with the common name of Black-eyed Susan. Tetrathecas are small shrubs with purple, pink or sometimes white flowers with black centres. Main flowering period is during spring, and the pendent flowers are cup- or bell-shaped.

Tetratheca thymifolia is one of the most successful species in cultivation, and is suitable for gardens or containers. It grows 50cm–1m in height by a similar width. The deep mauve-pink or white flowers are very showy, but with a slightly unattractive fragrance which is usually noticeable on hot days. Plants respond well to pruning after flowering. Sometimes suckers lightly.

Thomasia

This genus is one which is increasing in popularity as gardeners become more aware of the plants and their beauty. The slightly pendent flowers have a somewhat papery texture, and last well either in the garden, or as cut flowers.

Thomasia grandiflora is an outstanding ornamental. It grows 50cm–1m tall × 1–1.5m across, and has dark green leaves. The pink to mauve flowers, produced in spring, are around 3cm across, and are well-displayed on short stems.

Thomasia pygmaea is a low, spreading shrub of up to 50cm tall × 1–1.5m across. During spring it has a profuse display of mauve-pink flowers, attractively dotted with reddish tan. Flowers best in a sunny or lightly shaded garden position. Also does well in containers.

Thryptomene

Perhaps best known as a cut-flower, thryptomene is used extensively by florists both in Australia and overseas.

Thomasia grandiflora

Thryptomene calycina, Grampians Thryptomene is the species most widely grown for the cut-flower trade. It is a bushy shrub of 1.5–2.5m tall with profuse, small white flowers, which usually age to pink. These are produced over a long period from autumn to late spring. It likes moist soils but they must be very well-drained. Grows well in partial or full sun. Plants respond well to pruning or cutting of the flowers.

Thryptomene saxicola, Rock Thryptomene has pale to deep pink flowers during winter, and is the species most widely grown in private gardens. It is very adaptable, and tolerates a wide range of soil and climatic conditions. Plants grow to around 1.5m tall × 1–2m across, and regular light pruning will encourage bushy growth.

Westringia fruticosa
Coast Rosemary

This species is common in cultivation, and is adaptable to a wide range of soil and climatic conditions. It is a dense, bushy shrub which can grow 2–3m tall, by similar width, but responds well to pruning or regular clipping. White flowers marked with purple are produced mainly during spring, with scattered flowers at other times.

Clematis aristata

Climbers

Climbing and twining plants are useful for providing foliage cover against fences and walls, especially in places where there is insufficient space for wide-spreading trees or shrubs. They can also be used for covering unsightly structures or, if they are not too vigorous, for simply twining through other plants to give added foliage cover and variation, as well as floral beauty.

Some Australian climbing plants are light twiners and others vigorous climbers which are suitable only for growing as broad area groundcovers or on some form of sturdy support.

None of the plants listed will grow on walls or fences without a framework such as wire or slats around which they can twine. The following species are all suitable for cultivation in temperate to subtropical regions. There are also numerous climbing plants from the tropical areas of Australia, and information about these species will be found in *Climbing Plants in Australia*, see the Further Reading section.

Billardiera

This is an Australian genus of around 25 species, most of which are light twining or climbing plants. In addition to having attractive flowers, some also have decorative fruits.

Billardiera bicolor, Painted Billardiera grows 1–3m tall. The flowering period can be from spring through to early winter, when cream to yellowish flowers with dark purple stripes are produced in loose clusters.

Billardiera longiflora, Purple Apple-berry grows 2–4m tall. The tubular, greenish yellow flowers produced during spring are attractive to nectar-feeding birds, and they are followed by oblong, shiny fruits which are commonly bright purple. Prefers moist soils.

Billardiera ringens, Chapman River Climber is a slender-stemmed climber, with clusters of orange to bright red flowers, produced mainly during spring and summer.

Chorizema diversifolium

Chorizema is a genus of low shrubs and twiners belonging to the pea family. This species is a light twining plant which provides a showy display of orange, yellow and pink to purple pea-flowers, during spring. It grows best in an open to semi-shaded situation, with soils which are moist, but well-drained.

Cissus antarctica
Water-vine

This vigorous, tendril-bearing, woody climber is grown mainly for its decorative foliage. The oval to heart-shaped, toothed leaves are 7–11cm long. Small, cream flowers are produced in summer, followed by small, black, globular fruits. It can be grown in gardens or containers, and is suitable for use as an indoor plant. Responds well to pruning.

Clematis

This is a genus which occurs in several countries, and is popular for garden cultivation.

Clematis aristata is a vigorous climber with dullish leaflets grouped in threes. White to cream, starry flowers are produced in profusion during spring to autumn, and on female plants are followed by white, feathery seed-heads. Grows best with a cool, moist root area. The closely allied **Clematis glycinoides** has glossy leaflets.

Clematis microphylla is also a dense and vigorous species which grows in a situation where it has its foliage exposed to sunshine. The starry flowers produced in winter to spring are cream to greenish. Very tolerant of a wide range of conditions, from coastal to inland.

Hardenbergia comptoniana

Hardenbergia

This member of the pea family is well known in cultivation.

Hardenbergia comptoniana, Native Lilac occurs in WA, and is a dense climber which produces racemes of lightly fragrant, bluish purple pea-flowers during spring. It suffers damage from heavy frosts and likes a warm, well-drained situation. A less vigorous, white-flowered form is sometimes available.

Hardenbergia violacea, False Sarsaparilla; Purple Coral-pea. This frost-hardy species occurs in the eastern states and South Australia and produces showy racemes of usually mauve-purple pea-flowers during late winter to spring. Less common flower colours include white and mauve-pink. In addition to the climbing forms of this species, there are also shrubby forms of 1–2m tall.

Hardenbergia violacea 'Happy Wanderer' is a very vigorous selection which flowers profusely, with long, purple racemes of pea-flowers during winter to early spring. It responds well to light or hard pruning.

Hibbertia
Guinea Flowers

Hibbertia is a genus of around 150 species, a small number of which are climbing or trailing species.

Hibbertia dentata, Trailing Guinea-flower is a relatively light climber, with fleshy young stems and branchlets which become woody as they age. The leaves are green and shiny, with new growth usually reddish. Bright yellow, open-petalled flowers to 4cm across are produced mainly during spring and summer. Suitable for gardens or containers, including hanging baskets.

Hibbertia scandens, Climbing Guinea-flower, can become fairly vigorous, as a climber or as a groundcover in open situations. If grown in a sunny situation it can flower throughout the year, with a peak in spring to summer. The open-petalled, strongly fragrant flowers are bright yellow, to about 7cm across. Excellent for coastal exposure.

Hoya australis

This trailing or twining plant can be slow-growing, and is suitable for gardens or containers. It has oval, dark green leaves, and during spring clusters of waxy, white, fragrant flowers are produced. Likes a protected, frost-free situation.

Jasminum suavissimum
Sweet Jasmine

Many gardeners are familiar with *Jasminum polyanthum*, the highly fragrant climber, known simply as Jasmine, which is a native of China. *Jasminum suavissimum* is from Qld and NSW and is a slender climbing or creeping plant which is self-layering. The white flowers, produced in spring to summer, are in small clusters of three to five, and their fragrance is pleasant, rather than overwhelming.

Kennedia

This is an Australian genus of around 15 species, all of which are of trailing, twining or climbing habit. Most tolerate light frosts, but damage may be severe from heavy frosts. A selection is included here, and details of other species can be found in publications listed in the Further Reading section.

Kennedia coccinea, Coral Vine is a quick-growing and very showy climber, but often with a life span of only two to four years. It is useful for initial quick growth in a garden. The flowering period is during spring, when there is a profuse display of deep pink, orange-red and yellow pea-flowers. Flowers best in a sunny situation.

Kennedia macrophylla. A strong to vigorous climber with oval to rounded leaflets of 5–6cm long. During spring to early summer, bright red with yellow pea-flowers are produced in racemes to 15cm long, from the leaf axils. Excellent for screening out unsightly views.

Kennedia rubicunda, Dusky Coral-pea is a vigorous to very vigorous species. It can be grown as a groundcover in open areas, or requires a sturdy framework if it is to develop as a climber. The egg-shaped leaflets grow to 15cm long, and large, dusky pink to dark red flowers are produced during spring to summer. The flowers of this, and the following species, are attractive to nectar-eating birds. **Kennedia nigricans**, which has black and greenish yellow flowers.

Pandorea

A genus of around eight species distributed in Australia, New Caledonia and Malaysia. Two are fairly widely cultivated.

Pandorea jasminoides, Bower Climber is a robust climber with fairly dense, dark green, shiny leaves. Flowering is mainly in summer and autumn, when trumpet-shaped flowers of around 2–4cm long and 5cm across, provide a showy display. They are commonly pink or white with a deep red throat, or can be white with a

Pandorea pandorana

pale yellowish throat. Can suffer from heavy frosts.

Pandorea pandorana, Wonga Vine. Although sometimes initially slow growing, this is a vigorous climber once established. The flowers, seen mainly in spring, are smaller than those of *P. jasminoides*, but are produced in abundance. They are commonly cream with a reddish throat, or can be white, yellow or brownish. This species is hardy to most frosts.

Selected named cultivars of both these species are available. All forms respond well to pruning.

Passiflora cinnabarina
Crimson Passionflower

A woody climber with wrinkled, dark green leaves and twining tendrils, and produces bright coppery red flowers to 5cm across, during spring to early summer. The rounded, green fruits are edible, but not generally regarded as palatable.

Passiflora aurantia has delightful flowers which are initially white and deepen to pinkish red. It is frost-tender.

Tecomanthe hillii
Tecomanthe

A vigorous climber from Queensland, and liking a warm to hot situation. It has spectacular rose pink to purplish tubular flowers, to 10cm long, which are produced mainly during winter to spring. Tolerates light frosts.

Allocasuarina torulosa

Trees

There are many hundreds, even thousands, of Australian native trees. A large number of these provide beauty in their form, growth habit, barks and trunks, foliage, flowers or fruits, but not all are suitable for garden cultivation.

Trees can grow to a large size and may become prominent or even dominant where they are planted. It is always worth considering the aesthetic impact they will have on an area, especially if your surrounds still retain some local vegetation. If this is the case, then seek to use local trees, rather than those from other places. In doing so you will enhance the unique Australian character of the area. For highly urbanised areas the choice is not as important, but you may still wish to include some trees which were known previously to occur in your locality. There are nurseries now which specialise in local plants and they should be able to provide suitable trees.

Particularly in small gardens it is important to choose trees which will not grow too large for the position in which they are planted. Trees which must be constantly lopped or pruned can be a nuisance and sometimes unsightly, and their removal can be both inconvenient and costly. The species chosen in this selection are trees which do not generally exceed 15m tall in cultivation. Some are considerably smaller.

While trees fulfil an important function in any garden, it should be borne in mind that the use of a large number of trees can create very shaded conditions, and lower the moisture content in the soil, so that other plants struggle beneath them. Trees planted too close to buildings can also cause problems because the roots absorb subsoil moisture and this can result in movement or cracking of the foundations.

Any large trees, and particularly those which are moisture-loving such as species of *Callistemon*, and *Melaleuca*, should not be planted in close proximity to agricultural drains, as their roots can enter perforated pipes or loose joints between pipes, and cause blockages.

Further information regarding the use of trees in a garden, will be found in The Provision of Shade on page 9.

Acacia
Wattle

There are many, many species from which we could choose here. Three particularly recommended wattles are included, and a wider range can be obtained from the specialised publications listed in Further Reading.

Acacia adunca, Wallangarra Wattle grows 4–8m tall × 3–5m across. The leaf-like phyllodes are long, narrow and dark green, and during the flowering season, usually in mid winter to early spring, the tree can be almost covered with fluffy deep yellow, globular flower-heads. The flowers last for several weeks, and are not ruined by heavy rains, as occurs with some other species.

Acacia iteaphylla, Flinders Range Wattle. This is a commonly cultivated and ornamental species which can grow 3–5m tall by a similar width. Some forms are weeping, and others, which are low and spreading, are also available. The foliage is bluish green with pink to purplish new growth, and pale yellow flowers are produced during early autumn to spring. It has a tendency to regenerate readily, and therefore is not recommended for planting adjacent to bushland.

Acacia pravissima, Ovens Wattle. This is another highly desirable species for garden cultivation. It grows around 4–8m tall by a similar width and can have a weeping habit. The triangular phyllodes are small, and crowded along the branchlets. During winter the reddish flower-buds can be very attractive and these open in spring to provide a profuse display of bright yellow, globular flower-heads.

Agonis flexuosa
Willow Myrtle; Willow Peppermint

A tree of 8–15m tall which can spread 5–15m across. The leaves are long and narrow, hanging from the pendulous branchlets to give an attractive weeping habit. Small, white flowers are produced in clusters along the branchlets during spring to early summer. Highly recommended for coastal areas. Mainly frost-tender when young. There are a number of very attractive dwarf selections available.

Allocasuarina
She-oaks

This genus was established in 1982, grouping together a number of species which were previously included in *Casuarina*. They are cone-producing plants, characterised by their apparently leafless branchlets, with leaves having been reduced to 'leaf-teeth' which encircle the branchlets at intervals. Male and female flowers are usually produced on separate plants.

Allocasuarina torulosa, Forest Oak. This ornamental, fairly upright tree can grow 8–25m tall, but although often initially quick-growing, takes many years to exceed 10m in cultivation. It has pendulous foliage, which can be green or reddish to almost black. The flowers on female plants are small and produced along the stems, adding rusty to dark brown tones during autumn to early winter.

Allocasuarina verticillata, Drooping She-oak is a pendulous tree of 4–11m tall with dark, furrowed bark on the erect trunk. The yellow to brown male flowers can provide an attractive display during autumn to late spring.

Angophora costata
Smooth-barked Apple

Angophora is a close relative of the eucalypts, but without bud-caps covering the flowers. This beautiful species is noted particularly for its trunk, which has smooth, grey older bark which is shed to reveal new bright orange-brown to pink-brown bark. Plants can grow 10–25m tall, but in cultivation they are rarely more than 15m tall. White to cream flowers are produced in profuse, dense clusters during late spring and summer.

Banksia integrifolia
Coast Banksia

Several species of *Banksia* grow as small to medium trees. All are very decorative in flower and it is necessary to ensure that they are suited to the conditions available. Many must have well-drained, deep, sandy soils for survival. *Banksia integrifolia* grows well in such conditions, but will also tolerate heavier soil types. It can grow 10–20m tall, but will take many years to achieve these dimensions. The toothed leaves of 5–15cm long have a silvery undersurface which is decorative as the foliage is moved by the wind. Yellow flower-spikes of 5–15cm long are produced over a long period, with the main flowering being from autumn to early spring.

Callistemon
Bottlebrushes

Reference is made to the beauty and adaptability of callistemons in the section on Shrubs on page 30. The following are two of several species which grow to tree proportions.

Callistemon salignus, Willow Bottlebrush; Pink Tips can grow 5–15m tall × 3–5m across, but rarely exceeds 8m high in cultivation. It has whitish to cream, somewhat papery bark and the new foliage growth can be bright pink to red. Flower-spikes of white or pink to pinkish red are seen mainly in spring to early summer. Hardy to most frosts.

Callistemon viminalis, Weeping Bottlebrush is an extremely variable species, with several forms and named cultivars available having heights ranging from 1m–12m. Most plants grown from seed develop into small trees with a graceful, weeping habit, while selected lower-growing forms must be propagated from cuttings or tissue culture to retain the desired characteristics. The flower-spikes are bright red and can be produced throughout most of the year, with peak flowering in spring and autumn. Heavy frosts can damage plants.

Ceratopetalum gummiferum
NSW Christmas Bush

A bushy tree of 3–10m tall. Small, white flowers are produced in spring, but the main beauty of this species occurs later as the petals drop, and the starry calyx enlarges to become bright red. This provides a showy and long-lasting display during summer and early autumn. There are also some small-growing selections available, including 'Alberry's Dwarf Form'.

Elaeocarpus reticulatus
Blueberry Ash

This species commonly grows around 5–8m tall, although it can have a height of up to 15m in nature. Racemes of delicately fringed, white or pink flowers are produced during spring, and these are followed by oblong, dark blue berries of around 1cm long, which remain on the plants through to late winter. It is an adaptable plant which will grow well in a situation from full shade through to full sun, although it prefers some shade.

Eucalyptus ficifolia

Eucalyptus
Eucalypts

Eucalyptus is the largest and most significant genus of Australian trees, with over 750 species. They are sometimes referred to as gum trees, however there are several common names applied to plants in different categories, e.g. mallees, ironbarks, stringybarks, etc., and it is some of the smooth-barked species to which the term 'gum' correctly refers.

Eucalypts are of varying sizes, ranging from only 1m tall, to the world's largest hardwood trees of around 100m. Many are too large for normal garden use in city or suburban areas, but this still leaves a wide range of species in the small to medium size group, which are very popular garden trees.

A selection of seven species is included here, and readers requiring further information are referred to the specialised publications included in the Further Reading section.

Eucalyptus caesia. A decorative small tree whose most commonly cultivated form is the subspecies *magna*, which is often marketed as 'Silver Princess'. It grows 5–10m tall and the reddish branchlets, buds and fruits are covered with a whitish, powdery bloom. Plants can be weeping in habit. During winter to spring there is a showy display of large, pink to reddish flowers tipped with gold. Plants like a warm, well-drained situation, but can grow very quickly and become unstable in strong winds. They respond well to careful pruning. The smaller-flowered ssp. *caesia* is more slender, usually lacks strongly pendulous branches, and is very attractive.

Eucalyptus conferruminata, Bushy Yate. A densely foliaged tree of 5–10m tall, adaptable to a wide range of conditions, especially coastal exposure. Large clusters of yellow-green flowers are produced during winter to early summer.

Eucalyptus ficifolia, Red-flowering Gum. This species is well-known for its spectacular flowers of white, pink, scarlet or deep red, produced during summer to early autumn. It produces a dense canopy and can grow 6–15m tall. It likes a warm, well-drained situation, preferring deep, sandy soils, but will also grow in heavier types.

Eucalyptus forrestiana, Fuchsia Gum. This species is distinctive, as it is the buds and fruits, rather than the flowers, which are the eye-catching feature. It is a bushy, small tree of 4–6m tall with bright orange to red buds and fruits which hang from the branches throughout most of the year. The flowers are yellow, and seen from summer to late autumn. Grows best in a warm to hot, sunny situation in relatively low rainfall regions.

Eucalyptus leucoxylon* ssp. *megalocarpa, Large-fruited Yellow Gum. An extremely popular garden tree of 4–9m tall. It has a smooth trunk with attractive cream to greyish bark, and a light canopy of bluish green to deep green leaves. Flowers can be produced over a long period from autumn to early summer, and can be white, cream, yellow or pink to reddish.

Eucalyptus macrandra, Long-flowered Marlock grows 5–10m tall, and has a smooth, brown-grey trunk with bright green to blue-green foliage. Large clusters of yellowish green flowers are produced during summer to early autumn.

Eucalyptus scoparia, Wallangarra White Gum. This species grows 8–12m tall, with an attractive, smooth, whitish to grey trunk and a pendulous crown of narrow, weeping leaves. Small, white flowers are produced in clusters during late spring to early summer.

Hymenosporum flavum
Native Frangipani

This is an upright tree of 5–10m tall with horizontal branches and shiny, dark green leaves. The yellow and cream flowers, produced during spring to early summer, are tubular to about 3cm long, with flared petals, and gain purplish tonings as they age. They are highly fragrant. Likes a warm situation with full or partial sun. May suffer from frost damage when very young.

Eucalyptus leucoxylon ssp. *megalocarpa*

Lagunaria patersonii
Norfolk Island Hibiscus

This species is commonly a small to medium, cone-shaped, densely foliaged, single-trunked tree of 5–10m tall in cultivation. It is widely grown and is ideal for coastal situations. Pink, open-petalled flowers to 6cm across are produced during summer and autumn.

Lomatia fraxinifolia
Lomatia Silky Oak

This species is native to the rainforest regions of north-eastern Qld. It grows to about 10m tall, and has decorative, shiny, dark green, divided leaves with a pale undersurface. Creamy white flowers are produced in short racemes during summer to early autumn. Likes a warm, moist situation. Has potential for indoor use.

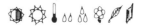
Lagunaria patersonii

Melaleuca
Honey-myrtles; Paperbarks

There are several of the taller-growing *Melaleuca* species which are widely grown in gardens and parks, and also as street trees. Some attain considerable size, and are moisture-loving. These species should not be grown where the roots can enter drainage pipes, or blockages can occur. Most species respond well to pruning, and are suitable for regular clipping or hedging, if desired. The following are commonly available from nurseries.

Melaleuca armillaris, Bracelet Honey-myrtle can grow 4–8m tall and is relatively upright in habit. It is widely used as a screening and windbreak plant. It has narrow, bushy, dark green leaves to 2.5cm long, and cream flower-spikes, produced mainly in spring to summer. For longevity it is best grown on a single trunk.

Melaleuca linariifolia grows 5–10m tall and is frequently seen as a street tree. It has whitish, papery bark and a crown of green leaves which can be almost covered by profuse clusters of white, feathery flowers, in late spring to summer.

Melia azedarach var. *australasica*
White Cedar

This is a deciduous species, which usually grows around 6–8m tall. It produces small, sweetly fragrant, purple and white flowers during spring to early summer. These are followed by greenish berries which become yellow to orange as they mature and are retained on the plants during winter, when the branches are leafless. It prefers a warm, relatively well-drained situation.

Pittosporum phylliraeoides
Butterbush

This *Pittosporum* is an upright tree of 3–6m tall, which will grow well in a variety of situations, including harsh, dry conditions. It has fragrant, small yellow flowers during late winter to spring, and these are followed by small, yellow fruits. It does not spread to become a bushland weed, as can happen with *Pittosporum undulatum*, Sweet Pittosporum.

Melaleuca linariifolia

Schefflera actinophylla
Umbrella Tree

A tree to 6m tall which grows well in tropical and subtropical regions, and can be grown as an indoor plant in cooler areas. The foliage is decorative with up to 16 leaflets each to around 30cm long, being produced in umbrella-like circles. During spring to autumn small red flowers are produced in long racemes, which are grouped at the branchlet tips. Responds well to light or harsh pruning. This species has a vigorous root system, and should not be planted close to underground pipes or paved areas.

Stenocarpus sinuatus
Firewheel Tree

A popular tree, due primarily to the spectacular, wheel-like formations of bright red flowers produced from late summer to winter. It is of upright habit, usually growing to around 6–15m tall, with large, shiny, dark green leaves. Grows best in a warm, frost-free situation. Can take many years to flower.

Syzygium
Lilly-pilly

Lilly-pillies are commonly cultivated trees, grown mainly for their showy displays of succulent, white, pink to purple or red berries. They are in the closely related genera of *Acmena*, *Eugenia* or *Syzygium.* Generally they are hardy to light frosts.

    Syzygium oleosum, Blue Cherry. Blue Lilly-pilly grows 5–10m tall with shiny, dark green leaves, and globular pink to bluish purple fruits seen in autumn to late winter. Previously known as *S. coolminianum*.

    Syzygium paniculatum, Magenta Cherry is a densely foliaged plant which responds well to pruning and is suitable for hedging or similar purposes. It can grow 5–9m tall, and is usually of upright habit. It produces

Pittosporum phylliraeoides

small, white flowers in summer, and the globular fruits are magenta in colour.

Tristaniopsis laurina
Kanooka or Kanuka; Water Gum

This species usually grows around 3–15m tall in cultivation, but it can become larger after many years, and can also become wide spreading. It has smooth, deciduous, cream to grey bark and shiny green leaves which are often initially reddish. During late winter to summer it produces an attractive display of clustered yellow flowers.

Xanthostemon chrysanthus
Golden Penda

A spreading tree to around 12m tall (but often may reach only 6m) with shiny, dark green leaves to 18cm long. During autumn there is a showy display of golden yellow flowers, with small petals and prominent stamens produced in clusters at the branchlet tips. Likes moist soils and a warm to hot situation.

The cultivation needs of Australian plants

Australia is a country with a very wide range of natural habitats and this has led to tremendous diversity in the natural plant life. This means that not all Australian plants can be expected to survive and thrive in each and every garden throughout the country.

It is extremely important that we try to learn a little more about the plants we hope to grow. We can find out the soil and climatic conditions they prefer, or we can seek to learn whether they come from dry inland regions, tropical rainforests of Queensland or snow-covered mountains of New South Wales, Victoria or Tasmania.

Climatic conditions

In gardening we should always attempt to work with nature as much as possible, rather than against it. Firstly we need to make the most of the conditions we have, and choose plants that are naturally suited to our climate and soils. This forms the basis of good gardening, and is the most practical in terms of maintenance time and expense.

The planting of local (or indigenous) native plants is now becoming increasingly popular, as we realise the value of the preservation and conservation of our environment, and often we find there are some very attractive species local to our particular area. Many of these plants are excellent for garden use, but in previous times were ignored, and regarded as 'bush plants' rather than species with horticultural potential.

If you wish, the climatic zones in your garden can be modified to some extent, often with minimal expense. One of the easiest ways to achieve this is through the planting of trees or shrubs specifically for the purpose of providing shade, or a screen for protection from wind, frost or other elements such as salt-laden coastal spray. These topics are all covered in detail on pages 9–13.

Soils and soil improvement

Very few Australian gardens have what can be loosely described as first class garden soils. It is often said that 'the grass on the other side of the fence is always greener', and the same concept is certainly true of garden soils. Those who live in sandy areas look with envy at the nutrient-rich, heavier soil types while those who attack the heavier soils with pick and shovel think those living in sandy regions have all the advantages. The truth is of course that both heavy and light soil types have their good and bad points, and with a little effort, both can be improved to produce the good, friable growing medium that makes gardening so enjoyable.

Heavy clay soils

Clay soils are composed of very fine particles which pack closely together, hindering water movement through to the subsoil, and causing sloppy, waterlogged conditions near the surface. In dry periods, the surface area can set hard, and be marked by minor or severe cracking. Neither situation is good for plant growth, although the actual clay may be quite rich in nutrients.

What is needed is to make the clay more friable, and this can be done in several ways.

Gypsum (hydrated calcium sulphate) makes little or no alteration to the nutrient value of soils, but if cultivated into clays causes the fine particles to group together into small clusters, thus allowing better penetration of both air and moisture through the soil. Gypsum is available from most garden suppliers, and the recommended rate for application is 1–1.5kg per square metre. Gypsum usually contains some heavy metals such as cadmium, and is therefore not recommended for areas which will be producing edible vegetables or fruits.

Compost and other organic materials such as leaf litter can also help to 'open up' clay soils, and make them more friable. The addition of such materials is highly recommended. Coarse river sand will also help achieve this purpose, but large quantities are required, and the expense involved can be prohibitive.

Cultivation of clay soils should be undertaken, wherever possible, by hand digging.

If the area to be cultivated is large, then a tractor (large or small) with a ripper blade should be used in order to break up the subsoil. The use of a rotary hoe should be avoided, as the rotating action of the blades can cause a hard pan base to form beneath the finely cultivated topsoil layer. This can lead to poor drainage and plant roots may have difficulty in penetrating the compacted layer.

Poor drainage can be a problem in areas of heavy soil, and this topic is dealt with later in this section.

Many plant species occur naturally in heavy clay or clay loam soils, and are therefore a logical choice if you are looking for plants able to grow well in such situations.

Light, sandy soils

Sandy soils are certainly much easier to cultivate than clays, but the major problem with sand is that often water drains readily, without there being sufficient moisture retention to supply the long-term needs of the plants.

Fine sand can also become water-repellent if it dries out, so that subsequent rainfall or supplementary watering will simply lie in puddles on the top, or run off, rather than penetrating.

Erosion from wind and water is a further problem in sandy regions.

One of the best methods of improving sandy soils is to add compost, leaf mould, aged animal manures or other organic matter. This will help improve the soil structure and moisture retention and also raise the nutrient value of the soil. Mulching is also very important as it can help to prevent erosion, as

Plants suitable for heavy clay soils

Plant names asterisked are discussed in detail in the text.

Acacia salicina (Native Willow)
  4–10m × 3–8m
Allocasuarina torulosa
Anigozanthos flavidus
Astartea fascicularis
Baeckea linifolia (Weeping Baeckea)
  1–3m × 0.5–2m
Banksia spinulosa
Brachychiton acerifolius (Flame Tree)
  usually 10–20m tall
Brachyscome multifida
Brachysema praemorsum
Callistemon — bottlebrushes
  'Burgundy' 2–4m × 2–4m
  phoeniceus red flowers
    2–4m × 3–5m
  salignus
  viminalis
Calothamnus quadrifidus
Eucalyptus
  leucoxylon ssp. *megalocarpa*
  macrandra
Grevillea
  'Clearview David' 2–3m × 2–4m
  confertifolia Grampians Grevillea
    to 50cm × 3m
  'Poorinda Firebird' 1.5–3m
    × 1.5–3m
Helichrysum apiculatum
Homoranthus papillatus
Hymenosporum flavum
Leptospermum macrocarpum (Copper
  Sheen Tea-tree) 1.5–2.5m × 1.5–2.5m
Melaleuca thymifolia
  violacea
  viridiflora 8–18m × 4–10m
Patersonia occidentalis
Pratia pedunculata
Scaevola 'Mauve Clusters'
Tristaniopsis laurina

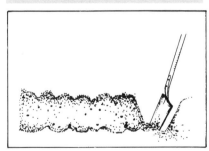
Hand digging

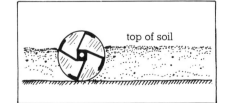
Rotary hoeing

well as being a source of organic matter. The practice of using tightly packed, slender, leafy branches which are kept in place by tautly-strung fencing wire has proved successful in combating erosion on sandy slopes. Also·protection from sand-blasting is given to young plants.

Sandy soils are commonly low in plant food value, because nutrients have been leached out as the water passes through. Many Australian plants have adapted to cope with this situation and are very efficient in their use of available nutrients, but others can suffer from nutrient deficiencies if soil improvement is not undertaken.

Despite the difficulties associated with sandy soils, a wide range of extremely attractive Australian plants grow naturally in deep, sandy soils, and will therefore thrive in such conditions. Many of these plants come from the sandy regions of south-western Australia, a region renowned for its magnificent wildflowers; while South Australia, Victoria, Tasmania, New South Wales and Queensland also have some very desirable and adaptable garden plants originating from sandy zones.

Acid and alkaline soils

Many people become confused by the acidity or alkalinity of soils, and technical terms such as a pH scale. In simple terms, very acid soils are found in moist, peaty areas, while alkaline soils, which have a high lime content, usually occur in arid or coastal regions. The pH scale is used to measure levels of acidity or alkalinity within the soil, and ranges from 4 — very strongly acidic, to 10 — very strongly alkaline.

Most Australian plants grow best in soils which are slightly acid, between pH 5.5 and pH 7, but there is also a considerable number which do well up to pH 7.5–7.8.

If plants are not growing well in your garden it could be worthwhile having the soil tested to determine the pH level. This is quite a simple procedure, which can be done with the aid of a small kit available from most of the larger nurseries, or your local nursery may be willing to test a sample for you.

If your soil has a pH reading of below 5, it is strongly acidic, and it is a relatively simple procedure to raise the pH level by the addition of dolomite lime or agricultural lime. This should be done by adding small amounts over a period of time and testing the pH level in between additions. Dolomite lime is recommended as a first choice, because overdosing with agricultural lime may cause problems which can result in poor growth.

Generally acidic soils do not pose many problems for cultivating Australian plants. Most plants which occur naturally in alkaline soils adapt well in acidic soils, but the reverse is not usually as successful.

If you have naturally alkaline soils, or garden soil to which too much lime has previously been added, you may have a pH reading of above 8. If this is the case, it can be a difficult task to lower the alkalinity without the possibility of damaging plants. The simplest method of coping with this situation is to select plant species which will tolerate the conditions available. However, the addition of well composted materials and the application of agricultural sulphur will help to overcome the problems. This will need to be a regular process until the desired pH level is reached.

A collage of low growing plants on a gently sloping, south-facing embankment, with a dense background of taller shrubs and trees. Plants included are *Stackhousia monogyna* (white-flowered, in foreground), *Grevillea saccata* (orange-red flowers), *Helipterum anthemoides* (white flowers), *Astartea* 'Winter Pink' and *Alyogyne huegelii* (purple flowers).

The magnificence of *Acacia boormanii* can be enjoyed during late winter to early spring, while the mottled trunk of *Eucalyptus maculosa* is forever changing its tones and textures.

For a splash of vivid spring colour *Chorizema cordatum* is hard to surpass. A wonderful plant, usually grown as a shrub, has the capacity to act as a semi-climber and is ideal if you let it take its own course amongst other shrubs in areas with dappled shade.

The small-flowered form of *Eucalyptus caesia*, although not as dramatic as the subspecies *magna,* is probably better suited to planting in confined areas.

Dampiera linearis is an exciting plant for the edge of paths, where it will flaunt its magnificent floral display during late spring and early summer. Yellow-flowered plants of *Conostylis* and *Hibbertia* are informally intermingled to create a pleasing picture.

Plants tolerant of alkaline soils

Plant names asterisked are discussed in detail in the text.

Acacia (Wattles)
  argyrophylla 3–4m × 4–6m
  calamifolia 2–5m × 2–4m
  harpophylla 10–20m × 4–10m
  *iteaphylla
  ligulata 2–5m × 4–7m
  melanoxylon 5–30m × 4–15m
  retinodes 4–8m × 3–7m
  sophorae 2–8m × 4–10m
*Agonis flexuosa
*Allocasuarina verticillata
*Alyogyne huegelii
Araucaria bidwillii Bunya Pine,
  30–50m × 10–20m
*Banksia integrifolia
Brachychiton populneus Kurrajong
  6–20m × 3–8m
*Callistemon 'Harkness'
  teretifolius 1–3m × 2–4m
*Cassia artemisioides
  nemophila 1–3m × 1–3m
Casuarina glauca Swamp Oak
  6–30m × 4–12m
*Clematis microphylla

*Correa alba
  *reflexa
*Eremophila glabra
  maculata 0.5–3m × 1–3m
Eucalyptus cinerea 8–18m tall
  cornuta 6–20m tall
  cosmophylla 4–10m tall
  *forrestiana
  *leucoxylon
  nutans 2.5–4m × 3–5m
  platypus 4–10m × 5–10m
  steedmanii 4–12m tall
Grevillea aquifolium 20cm–3m × 1–4m
  *lavandulacea
  *thelemanniana
*Hakea francisiana
  petiolaris 3–6m × 2–4m
  scoparia 1.5–3m × 1.5–3.5m
  suaveolens 3–6m × 3–5m
*Lagunaria patersonii
Lasiopetalum behrii 1–2m × 1–2m
*Leptospermum lanigerum
*Melaleuca armillaris
  *decussata
  halmaturorum 4–6m × 2–4m
  lanceolata 3–8m × 2–6m
Myoporum floribundum 2–4m
  × 2–3m
  insulare 3–5m × 4–8m
*Pittosporum phylliraeoides
*Templetonia retusa

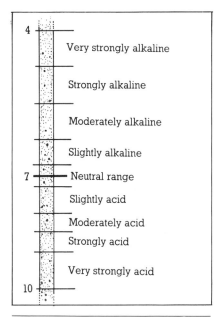

pH Scale

Basic garden drainage

Good drainage is one of the major features which should not be overlooked in basic garden planning and soil preparation. In areas of heavy soils, provision must be made for the dispersal of excess water, though not necessarily moving it off the property, while in arid, sandy zones, maximum use must be made of whatever natural water is available.

It is not easy to dig drains, or raise the level of a garden bed once planting has been completed. One of the simplest methods of improving drainage around garden areas is to build up the level of the beds, even if only by 15–20cm. This can be done using topsoil from a pathway, other areas of paving, reconstruction around the garden, or stockpiled from the house construction site. So much valuable topsoil remains beneath a house built on

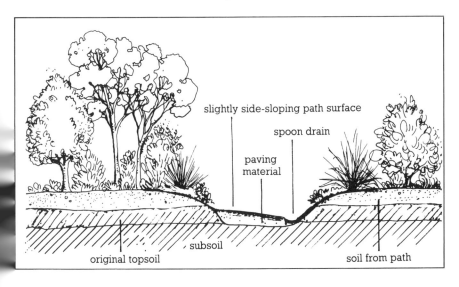

A surface drain. Any topsoil removed can be added to nearby gardens.

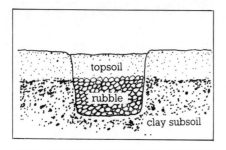

Rubble drain

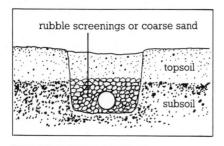

Agricultural drain, showing pipe surrounded by rubble screening or coarse sand.

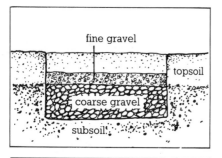

A soak pit

stumps, and it is a crying waste of a valuable resource to be left where it does not see the light of day. If you are planning to build, make sure all the topsoil which is likely to be covered by buildings is rescued before work is started.

A surface spoon drain can also be used to channel excess water in a desired direction, and this will also provide additional topsoil for use on garden beds. The further addition of compost or other organic matter may be all that is needed to raise the area sufficiently to provide good growing conditions for the plants.

A number of Australian plants will tolerate poor drainage, and in fact be extremely useful in reducing moisture levels in the soil. The symbol ⚶ in the plant descriptions indicates those species worth considering if you have a section in the garden which is wet for part or all of the year.

Rubble drains and agricultural drains can also be used as a means of removing excess water from a particular area. It is important to check the degree of fall in drains such as these, to ensure that they will work efficiently, gradually taking the water in the desired direction while also allowing it to seep into the subsoil. The gradient should be no greater than 1 in 250 to achieve this purpose. Alternatively you may wish to have a pool or bog garden into which the water can flow.

A small, reflective pool will provide many pleasant images and need be no more than 10cm deep. It can easily be constructed using heavy duty black plastic. Provided the edges are camouflaged, it will be most effective. If you wish to construct a pool of larger dimensions in a non-clay area, it is wise to refer to one of the many do-it-yourself publications or to seek the services of a landscape contractor.

Bog gardens can provide you with the opportunity to grow an extended range of plants not suited to the conditions in other areas of the garden. Bog garden plants require permanently moist soil. This can be done by digging a shallow pool in the subsoil, then refilling the excavation with topsoil, making sure that the upper surface of the soil is below the level of the surrounding area. Success in these gardens may not happen quickly, but you can have fun experimenting with a selection of plants which will tolerate waterlogging. Examples of small, carpeting or tufting plants are *Bauera rubioides* var. *microphylla*, *Goodenia humilis*, *Mazus pumilio*, *Patersonia occidentalis*, *Pratia pedunculata*, *Restio tetraphyllus*, *Selliera radicans* and *Viola hederacea*.

While moisture-loving plants are excellent for growing in poorly drained areas, those with the potential to become large should not be planted near agricultural pipes, as the roots can grow towards, and into, the water source, eventually clogging up the pipes and preventing good drainage.

It may be possible to direct excess water towards an easement or other larger drainage system. In areas which suffer from long periods of dryness it is much better to try and conserve the excess surface water. There are a number of ways this can be done. In well-drained soils a soak pit gradually disperses the water into the subsoil. A hole of around 1m square × 1m deep should be dug, and the subsoil replaced with coarse rubble in the lower two-thirds, followed by around 10cm of smaller gravel. This layer can be covered with a square of polyester fibre mesh, then the hole can be brought up to ground level using the removed topsoil. Such a pit should be constructed at least 3m away from the nearest building, particularly if drains are being directed towards this area. For areas which have shallow topsoil, a series of trenches to about 30–50cm deep, constructed in the same way, will be adequate.

A more informal treatment would be to construct a series of shallow soak pits of differing depths which could be designed to appear as a dry creek bed and become an integral part of your garden landscape.

Time of planting

Planting is an interesting and rewarding task, and if good results are to be achieved some basic guidelines are important for success. Soil preparation and weeding are the two most important preliminary tasks.

Planting can be done at any time, though generally the best times are mid-autumn or early to mid-spring. If planting before or during summer, supplementary watering may be needed and prior to winter frosts initial protection to safeguard new foliage may be required.

Planting techniques

Dig the planting hole. It should be approximately twice as wide as it is deep.

When buying plants ensure that the depth of the topsoil, in the area where planting, is greater than the depth of the container. If the topsoil is shallower, it is desirable to build the bed up with natural soil. Digging deeper into subsoil and filling it with lighter soil or potting mix can cause water to collect and waterlog the root system.

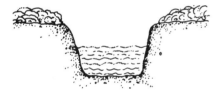

If the soil is dry, fill the hole with water and leave to drain away.

Ensure plant is thoroughly moist before removing it from container. If quite dry it can be placed in a bucket of water for around 30 minutes, then allowed to drain. A mixture of water and plant starter (a root stimulant) can be used to encourage initial root growth.

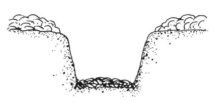

Make sure soil at the base of the hole is broken up with a spade or fork. Mound the loose soil slightly at the base of the hole, to allow the plant roots to point downwards and out from the centre.

Tip plant from the container.

Inspect carefully and make sure any weeds or weed roots are removed. If roots are coiled try to straighten them, or alternatively remove tightly coiled roots with clean, sharp secateurs. Remove also any dead or damaged roots. If there is a dense root-ball, gently tease out feeder roots from the sides, to encourage them to develop outwards from the central root area. Some disturbance of the root ball may occur, but try to avoid breaking the main root ball and releasing the soil to expose the whole root system.

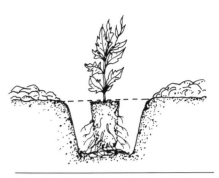

Place the plant in the hole, keeping the level of the potting mixture just minimally below that of the garden soil. Spread the roots evenly.

Fill the hole with soil. Add a small amount of fertiliser to the loose soil and mix thoroughly. Excessive use of fertiliser at planting can be detrimental, particularly if plants have been recently fertilised at the nursery.

Water gently but thoroughly, using at least half a bucket, (5 litres) of water per plant.

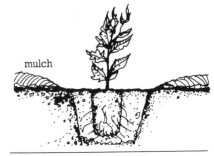

The area around the new plant can be mulched if desired. Further information on mulching is available on page 56.

Garden maintenance

Watering

Australia is the earth's driest habitable continent, with limited water catchment areas. Water is not an infinite resource and in many areas there is a real need for its conservation.

Gardening contributes significantly to our overall water use, and often the amount of water used in this way is considerably more than is necessary. Good garden planning should take into account natural rainfall levels and maximum use of the conditions available. Use supplementary watering only where necessary for particular plants or plant groupings.

How to reduce the need for watering

Many Australian plants have adapted to survive with a relatively small amount of moisture, and in many areas will survive on natural rainfall alone, once their root systems have become established. It is therefore desirable to group any plants requiring supplementary watering together in a garden, so that only these sections need watering by hand, hose or sprinkler systems during dry periods. It will save on both maintenance time and water wastage.

Mulching also reduces the need for supplementary watering in a garden. A mulch can help to reduce soil temperatures during hot weather, and also minimise moisture evaporation from the upper soil layer. Further discussion on mulching appears on page 56.

Plants which are regularly watered and fertilised will usually grow at a faster rate, and their need for water to support their new growth will be greater than those plants left to grow at a pace more natural for the species. We can then become caught up in a vicious cycle. The more we water, the more we need to continue to water, or plants can be lost.

Avoid watering on a hot day, even if plants are wilting. Wait until some time after the sun is no longer on the plants, or if possible, it is much better to delay watering until a cool spell of weather. This decreases the rate of evaporation and also the risk of encouraging fungal root diseases, which thrive in warm, moist conditions.

A good method of checking whether water is needed is to scratch or dig the soil to a depth of 2–3cm, or if you are still not certain, use a spade or fork to a greater depth. If it is moist, there is usually no need to water. There are a number of commercial products available for measuring the moisture content of soils and these may be useful for some gardeners.

The question of how often a garden should be watered is one which perplexes many plant growers, and some find it difficult to realise that the answer may be 'never'. Young plants which have been in the garden less than six months may require either rainfall or supplementary watering once every two to three weeks. For well-established plants, a monthly watering may be adequate. Some will even cope quite well for several months on the moisture available in lower levels of the soil.

In areas where many plants are being grown in close proximity, soils can dry out more readily than where trees or shrubs are sparse. Other aspects

When to water

One difficulty commonly experienced by gardeners is knowing when plants require water.

Sometimes a plant's foliage will show signs of wilting when it is suffering from a lack of moisture. However, if this only applies to new tip growth, the soil should be checked for moisture content before watering. Often on hot days, the roots of young, rapidly growing plants are simply not able to take in moisture at a level sufficient to maintain the thirsty new growth, even though the soil is quite damp. In this situation, the leaves will usually recover quite well during the cool of the evening, and additional watering may not even be necessary.

likely to affect the situation include the amount of direct sunshine or drying wind which reaches the soil surface.

Sometimes gardeners feel that to neglect the regular watering of a garden is the same as neglecting to feed their children, but there is really very little similarity. Many Australian plants are killed by over-watering.

How to water correctly

One of the great dangers in plant watering is to water lightly at frequent intervals. This only moistens the upper soil layer, and the root system develops mainly in the region of the soil where water is available. It is also the section of soil which dries out first if watering is not maintained. If the plant has insufficient roots to penetrate into lower levels, death may result.

Deep soaking encourages the roots to develop to a lower level within the soil, and the plant then has a much greater chance of survival during any extended dry period. Deep soaking can be achieved quite simply through the use of a perforated soaker hose, or by allowing a normal hose to gently trickle on the garden bed, moving it around every hour or so. Trickle irrigation systems can also be installed and will achieve the same purpose.

Sinking short, broad pipe lengths vertically into the ground around trees is often very useful for watering, particularly during extended dry periods. They can be filled with water, which can then soak gradually into the soil.

If using a hose which has been left attached to a tap, always check that the water is cool before directing it onto foliage of a plant. On a summer's day water from a hose can be extremely hot at first, and can severely burn, or in some cases kill, small plants.

Watering should always be done with care, whether from a bucket or a hose. A large quantity of water dumped carelessly on the base of a plant, or a strong spurt from a hose, can dislodge soil around the stem and expose some of the small feeder roots. This can be particularly damaging to young plants, and certainly doesn't help the development of older ones.

Fertilising

All plants require nutrients to grow healthily. These are obtained from air, water and the soil.

In many cases sufficient quantities are available from these sources without the additional application of plant fertilisers, but in some instances soils may be low in nutrients and we can top-up the supply to help maintain good plant growth.

Plants obtain carbon, oxygen and hydrogen from air and water. The other elements essential to their development are nitrogen (N), phosphorus (P) and potassium (K). These are naturally available in most soils, and are contained in various proportions in commercially prepared fertilisers. This ratio is usually indicated on the packet, e.g. N:P:K: — 18:2:8.

Nitrogen is important for good foliage growth, while phosphorus and potassium are valued for encouraging stem and root development, as well as flowering and fruiting.

Some Australian plants, particularly species from very poor soils, have adapted to be very efficient in their use of whatever phosphorus is available, and can therefore suffer adversely if an excess of this nutrient becomes available. A range of fertilisers with low phosphorus levels, specifically for use with Australian plants, is now obtainable from many nurseries and garden centres.

Other elements usually available in the soil are sulphur (S), calcium (Ca), iron (Fe), magnesium (Mg), manganese (Mn), zinc (Zn), copper (Cu), boron (Bo), chlorine (Cl), molybdenum (Mo) and cobalt (Co). In certain circumstances plants can become deficient in one or more of these elements, and they can be applied through specific products available from nurseries. Beware of using over-dosages, as it can be very difficult to rectify the problem.

Well-trained nursery staff can usually recognise the symptoms of different nutrient deficiencies, often shown by abnormal colourings in the foliage, and can suggest suitable products for use. There are also publications dealing specifically with the topic of plant nutrition, available from bookshops or libraries.

In general, if your Australian native plants look healthy and vigorous there is no need to apply fertilisers.

A light application of a slow-release fertiliser can be used in early spring each year, if you wish, to help maintain good growth and vigour, but plants should never be forced by excessive fertilising, particularly if you are looking for good, long-term results. Fertilisers promote growth of all plants, and weeds are no exception, so beware!

Frequent use of liquid fertilisers designed to give a rapid burst of growth is not recommended, except in the case of annuals or other plants where short-term results are desired. However, such fertilisers can at times be useful for correcting deficiencies.

Animal manures should be allowed to age before use, and can then be valuable in general soil improvement (see page 46), as well as being a rich source of nutrients. The introduction of unwanted weeds can be a problem which follows the use of some animal manures.

If using fertilisers, always read the packet thoroughly before use, not later. For most fertilisers, the soil should be moist at the time of application. Use the products according to directions given, and in the quantities specified or less, never more. Half of the recommended dosage rate stated on packages is usually ample for most Australian plants. The number of Australian plants which have died in gardens from over-fertilising would far outweigh those which have died from lack of sufficient nutrients.

Cultivating

Many growers of vegetables, annuals and other plants which benefit from regular cultivating, are often unsure how to best care for the soil around their Australian plants.

While good soil preparation prior to planting is strongly recommended regular digging or hoeing is usually not required, and indeed for species with root systems which are fairly close to the surface, it can have undesirable effects.

Weeds should be removed from around plants, using no more digging than is necessary to ensure that their roots are also removed.

If the soil in the garden has been compacted, a light hoeing or forking can be beneficial, as it helps to make air more available to the plant roots. The addition of a mulch is recommended. Mulching helps to alleviate compaction, which, in areas not subjected to foot and vehicular traffic, is most commonly caused by rain or watering from sprinklers.

Weed control

Unwanted plants compete with those we treasure for moisture, nutrients and sunlight. A good thorough removal of all weeds and weed roots from an area during initial soil preparation and prior to planting is a great start on the road to weed elimination. Ongoing maintenance weeding may then involve the removal of seedlings which germinate in the area, before they flower and seed. There is an oft-quoted phrase 'One year's seeding gives seven years weeding', and it can be true!

What is a weed?

Generally plants which are regarded as weeds are those which grow well in a wide range of unchosen situations, and compete vigorously with other plants. Garden plants can also become weeds and escape into our bush areas to compete with the local vegetation, if given the right soil and climatic conditions. In various areas of Australia several well-known plants should be treated with great caution. In most cases it would be best not to grow them at all. These include the showy yellow-flowered boneseed and brooms, coprosma, holly, ivy, lantana, ochna, pampas-grass and wandering jew.

Some Australian plants have also proved invasive when cultivated outside the area where they naturally occur. These include species of *Acacia*, particularly the cootamundra wattle, *Acacia baileyana* and *Acacia longifolia*, sallow wattle, *Hakea salicifolia*, *Leptospermum laevigatum*, *Melaleuca hypericifolia*, *Pittosporum undulatum* and *Sollya heterophylla*.

If you live near areas of natural bushland you should be particularly aware of introducing problem plants which could prove difficult to control. You should remove immediately any species in your own gardens which show this tendency.

Weed removal

Weeds can be removed manually, with a two-pronged weed remover, a small fork, or a hand-hoe. It is important with any perennial weeds that as much of the root as possible should be removed. Some species such as couch grass, kikuyu, oxalis and sorrel have the capability to re-grow from even small sections of root left in the soil, and in these cases total removal is desirable.

The 'Bradley Method of Weed Control' is a method of manual weeding, developed for use in larger areas of weed infestation, such as in natural bushland. Its basic principles involve disturbing the soil as little as possible; avoiding an increase in weed development by not tackling an area greater than can be given follow-up attention; and encouraging the development or regeneration of other desirable plants in the area. A publication on this particular method of weed control is obtainable, and details are included in the Further Reading list at the conclusion of this book.

Weeds can also be treated chemically, with the use of herbicides. This is less desirable than manual removal, but herbicides can be of use, and very effective, if all other methods fail. Preference should be for biodegradable products such as glyphosate, which is usually sold as 'Zero' or 'Roundup', and is neutralised on contact with soil. Long-term, residual compounds should not be used, unless absolutely necessary.

Herbicides should always be used with utmost caution, and instructions on the label adhered to strictly. Herbicides should never be sprayed on a windy day, as a number of them are not selective and your plants may suffer damage or die. The use of protective clothing is advisable, and always wash thoroughly after handling any herbicide or other garden chemical.

Weed prevention

It is not always possible to prevent the introduction of weeds into your garden, particularly if you live near areas where weeds are allowed to grow unchecked, and seeds are brought in by wind, birds or other means. There are however, some points you can keep in mind to reduce any weed problem.

- Avoid using animal manures which are likely to contain weed seeds.
- Do not add to your compost bin any material containing weed seeds or live creeping roots of weeds such as couch, kikuyu or sorrel.
- Do not buy plants from nurseries which can be seen to have a major weed problem in the pots or surrounding garden beds. Pots can look weed-free, but may contain numerous weed seeds, and also weed roots may have been left below the potting mix surface if weeding has been superficial.

  If you particularly want a plant which you know is infested with weeds, carefully wash all the soil from the roots and re-pot the plant into a clean, new mix. Allow the plant to become re-established in the container (initially in a protected site), before planting it out into the garden.
- Mulching can assist in weed prevention by smothering soft plants such as annuals, and reducing seed germination. In cases where seeds do germinate in the mulch, they can often be removed fairly easily if this is done before they penetrate down into the topsoil.

Mulching

Mulching

A mulch is a layer of organic or inorganic material placed on a garden bed, or a groundcover plant which provides a living mulch.

The aim of using a mulch is to assist in plant development and in general maintenance within the garden. Mulches will reduce evaporation of moisture from the soil during hot, dry periods, help prevent soil compaction, reduce soil temperature fluctuations and also assist in weed control.

Inorganic Mulches

The inorganic materials of coarse sand, gravel or crushed rock provide excellent mulches, but can be expensive to obtain. Fine sand is not as good as coarser material, as it can become water-repellent if it dries out. It can also provide excellent conditions for seed germination, although seedlings can be easily removed if noticed while they are still young. The recommended depth for sand and gravel mulches is around 5–7.5cm.

Organic Mulches

A number of organic materials are commonly used for mulching, including woodchips, pinebark, leaves and twigs broken up in mulch-cutters, bush litter, sawdust, wood shavings, lawn clippings, compost and straw. All these materials can be effective as mulches, although they will break down in time, and may need replacement.

These organic mulches are commonly used at a depth of 2–10cm. Mulches which are too deep can prevent water from reaching the soil, because mulch absorbs large quantities of water.

Organic mulches should never be placed right against the trunks of plants, as collar-rot can occur. Fresh organic material can also become quite warm during the breaking-down process, and this can have an adverse effect on plants if it is piled against the trunks.

As materials such as sawdust decompose, nitrogen is absorbed from the soil, and some yellowing of plants being grown in the vicinity may be seen. This can be corrected by a light application of hoof and horn, or a slow-release nitrogen fertiliser. Sawdust or shavings from treated timbers should not be used, as the chemicals can have an adverse effect on plant growth.

Sheet mulches

Layers of different materials are also sometimes used for mulching, particularly for the purpose of weed control. Newspaper, cardboard, carpet and underfelt can be effective.

Plastic sheeting, and similar materials such as rubber-backed carpets should be avoided, as they prevent the penetration of air and water to the soil, which can cause it to become sour, and topsoil can wash away in the run-off areas from the material. Plastic sheeting has, however, been used successfully on small areas around newly planted trees and shrubs. It is not recommended for wide-scale mulching.

Woven or knitted polypropylene fabric, which is now obtainable has some of the benefits of sheet plastic without the adverse effects referred to above, for weed control. It is available through nurseries.

Sheet mulches do not generally look attractive in a garden setting, and therefore a light cover of a suitable organic mulch is recommended.

Living Mulches

Groundcover plants can be very effective in providing a living mulch around larger shrubs and trees. Even though they do take a degree of moisture from the soil, their effectiveness in reducing evaporation and cooling the topsoil during warm weather, makes their planting for this purpose most worthwhile.

Groundcovers have the benefit of increasing in effectiveness as they grow and spread, while organic mulches break down. Therefore a combination of initial mulching with organic materials, and the planting of groundcover species, can be very effective. A selection of Australian groundcover plants is provided on page 25.

Mulching in frost and fire-prone areas

Mulching as a means of frost protection has been quite a common practice in the past. While inorganic mulches can provide a warmth retention barrier above the soil level, organic mulches are less desirable, as they can absorb moisture which then freezes and reduces the temperature around the plants even further. Later, as they defrost, there is a release of latent heat which may damage plants. Organic mulches in areas of low temperature are therefore not recommended, and during winter, bare, uncultivated ground is regarded as one means of reducing frost damage to plants. In some areas the rolling of soil has proved beneficial by providing a flat surface, which eliminates pockets where frost can occur.

Organic mulches can also cause some problems in fire-prone regions. If a mulch such as a thick layer of sawdust or other flammable material is used and is within a burnt area, the mulch can continue to smoulder for several days below surface level, then break out perhaps some distance away. Similarly, if mulches of this nature are used, piles of garden refuse should never be burnt nearby. We should of course avoid burning garden refuse wherever possible, with the exception perhaps of any diseased material. Other leaves and branches can be cut for use as a mulch, or added to the compost bin.

Pruning

Pruning is very important if you wish to grow healthy and attractive native plants, yet is often neglected.

Most Australian plants respond extremely well to regular light pruning and this can make all the difference between plants which are vigorous and attractive, or ones which are untidy and sparsely foliaged. Of course there are always some plants which have a pleasant form or habit without being pruned, and in some instances, injudicious pruning will lessen their attractiveness.

In general terms, pruning can help to promote good growth, direct the plant's growth to suit the needs of the situation, and be used to encourage better flowering or fruiting. It should also be used to remove any dead, diseased or damaged sections of a plant.

Pruning Tools

The main tools used in plant pruning are secateurs for general use, and pruning saws for larger stems and branches. It is important that they be kept sharp, and that they be cleaned regularly, particularly if they have been used on any diseased plant material. Washing in a solution of household bleach or antiseptic is adequate.

Tip pruning

Tip pruning can be carried out with secateurs, or simply with the thumb and forefinger. It is done by removing the growing tip from a stem or branchlet, so that bushy growth then develops from sideshoots. Tip pruning can be done from the time a plant is only 15–20cm tall, depending on what you are hoping to achieve for its future development.

Tip pruning

Pruning a flowering stem.

Cutting to an outward pointing bud.

Tip pruning is a very effective form of regular, light pruning, which will certainly encourage bushy growth.

In nature, tip pruning occurs as caterpillars or larger animals eat out the soft, new leaf growth, or as it is damaged by frost, winds or hot sun. In the garden it can be done quite simply as we walk around the garden — at any time of the year.

General shrub pruning

A rule-of-thumb with general pruning of evergreen shrubs is that it is best done during or immediately after flowering.

The cutting of flowers for indoor decoration is one very effective means of pruning, to which most plants respond well. By pruning a plant after flowering we are not removing material which already contains buds for next season's flowers, and the plant has time to grow in the direction desired before the next buds form.

Plant pruning is very largely a matter of common sense. If we look at a stem we will see that leaves are joined at different points around it. It is from these points, or nodes, that the buds for new growth develop. We can choose the direction in which we want stems to emerge, then cut just above that node. The cut should be made on a slant so that water will run off, away from the developing bud, and not cause any deterioration.

In many species it is common for branches to be cut just above an outward-pointing bud, so that plants will not become inwardly crowded, with branches rubbing against each other. If on the other hand you are pruning a shrub away from a path, or for some other reason want to encourage its growth in a different direction, you can choose the bud from which new growth will best suit your needs.

For most species, plants should not be pruned back to leafless stems, as buds for new foliage growth may not be in that area of the plant. This is one of the reasons why regular light pruning is preferable to hard pruning once every four to five years. There are some plants which are exceptions to this rule, and readers who would like to know more about particular plants can find this information in *Pruning — A Practical Guide*, as listed in the Further Reading section.

Pruning of herbaceous plants

Some Australian herbaceous plants will benefit greatly from hard cutting on an annual basis, particularly plants in the Asteraceae or daisy family. Many of the low-growing, suckering species of *Brachyscome*, *Helichrysum*, and other daisy plants, will flower almost throughout the year, but if cut back to around 5cm above ground level in late autumn or winter, they will gain renewed vigour, retain a more attractive growth habit, and be ready to provide a new display of eye-catching flowers by spring or early summer.

Pruning of trees or large shrubs

As with general shrub pruning, the growth and development of trees and larger shrubs can be directed, as desired, from an early stage. Side branchlets can be removed to provide development on a clean trunk, or upper growth can be pruned to encourage a bushy habit.

The removal of branches from well-established, large plants requires considerable thought and planning in order to avoid undesirable damage to the plant, other plants or structures nearby, and of course, the person undertaking the work.

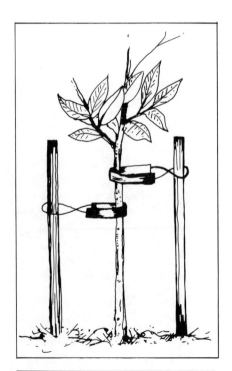

Multiple staking, using two stakes. Note protective covering around trunk.

Large branches may need to be secured with a rope or ropes before cutting, so that their fall can be controlled, and a ladder or similar piece of equipment may be needed to support the pruner. Ensure that all equipment is adequate to the task it is to perform. Pruning can then be undertaken as illustrated.

Staking

Australian plants grown in their permanent position from a very young stage rarely need the additional support of staking. However, stakes or guy-wires are sometimes needed for advanced plants transplanted from containers to the garden, or for particular plants which have grown quickly with topgrowth which has exceeded the rate of development of the root system.

When staking a plant which requires support, it is recommended that some movement of the trunk be allowed so a gradual strengthening will occur. If the plant is staked tightly this does not happen, and the plant will continue to be reliant on support.

The ties which attach a plant to a stake should always be of a broad, soft nature, rather than narrow string or wire which can damage bark and cut into the trunk. Damage is often evident from material used for nursery plant labels which has not been removed at planting.

For tying large plants, wire can be threaded through a length of plastic or rubber hose, which acts as a cushion between the wire and the bark.

Stakes should, if possible, be placed in the ground at the time of planting to avoid damaging plant roots later.

In many cases the use of two to four stakes will be more beneficial to the plant's development than one stake alone.

Staked plants should be checked on a regular basis to ensure that they are not being damaged by the ties, or by rubbing against the stakes. A check should also be made at the base of the plant, particularly in windy areas, as the plant can be blown around within the restraints of staking, forming a hole in the soil at the base of the trunk. If this happens, try and firm the soil around the trunk and secure the ties slightly, while still allowing some trunk movement. Usually within one or two months there are obvious signs of the base of the trunk swelling and becoming more stable.

Plant supports

Most Australian climbing plants require some form of support on which to grow. If they are being grown against a wall or fence, support can be provided quite simply by the use of a few nails and some string or wire. This can however, turn out to be a short-term solution only, unless durable materials are used. Rusting of wire or nails, or the rotting of string, can easily cause the plant to fall in a heap to the ground.

It is therefore recommended that if any form of plant support is being constructed, a little extra time and expense should be allowed, to ensure that the results will be lasting.

Any timber used should be naturally durable, or treated to ensure long life. Copper or galvanised wire and nails will not rust, and can therefore be expected to outlast other types.

Pruning large branches

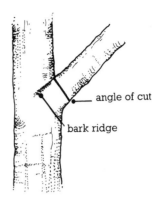

1. Make a shallow cut on the underside of the branch to be removed around 20cm from the trunk. This is important to avoid ripping of the bark and adjacent wood, which can also damage the trunk.

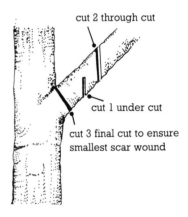

2. Cut and remove the branch, leaving a stub of around 30cm long. If the branch is long and heavy it is best to reduce it in sections.
3. With the weight of the branch no longer a problem, remove the excess from the trunk leaving a very small stub and the outer layers of the trunk intact.

ladybird

dragon fly

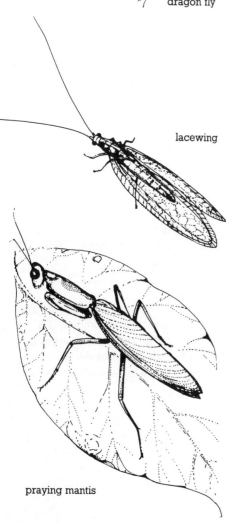

lacewing

praying mantis

Insects that are useful in the garden.

Plant guards

In certain circumstances, it is necessary to protect plants from natural elements such as strong winds, coastal exposure and frost; from being eaten by animals such as rabbits or kangaroos; or from damage which may be caused by dogs, cats, children, balls or other family activities.

Plant guards need not be fancy, they can be very simple and easy to construct. Chicken wire with a 2.5cm mesh cut into lengths and joined to form a cylinder is effective against most small animals. To protect against strong winds, 3–4 wire pegs pushed into the ground over the lowest parts of the mesh can stabilise the guards, or they can be buried into the ground to a depth of 5–7cm.

For small, temporary guards, three wooden stakes and a plastic bag can be adequate and do provide wind protection. Guards of ultra-violet resistant plastic will last much longer than untreated plastic.

Larger guards, which will need to last for extended periods, as well as perhaps cope with buffeting by grazing animals, can be made from stronger materials such as welded mesh fencing, used with strong, iron stakes.

With all types of plant guards, efforts should be made to ensure that the plant can develop as naturally as possible within the protection of the guard. As soon as a plant is sufficiently developed to grow well without further protection, the guard should be removed.

Pest control

In general, Australian plants don't suffer great devastation from pests. This is particularly true if you encourage native birds to the garden, as they form a very important link in the food chain, and in doing so devour many creatures commonly regarded as garden pests.

As discussed under the topic of Tip Pruning earlier in this chapter, caterpillars and other creatures which eat out the new tip growth of plants provide a natural form of pruning, which often does very little damage in the garden apart from encouraging a more bushy development.

It is therefore not necessary for you to regard every creature you find on your plants as a dangerous problem for which you must find an immediate solution.

Occasionally you will have an infestation of pests which exceeds the food needs of the birds in the area, and you can then assist in restoring the balance of nature by removing and squashing some of the offending creatures.

Some insects are very useful in a garden. Ladybirds are well known, the most common variety being a small, rounded, yellow to orange insect, with black spots on the wing covers. Their diet includes aphids, mealy bugs, mites and scales. Praying mantises are also helpful to have in the garden, and feed on a wide range of insects. They have a somewhat stick-like appearance, and can be recognised by their ability to turn their heads, which is uncommon in the insect world. You may also find their firm, sponge-like egg-cases or oothecas, attached to plants in the garden. Other creatures which can help to control pests in the garden include ants, ant lions, assassin bugs, predator beetles, dragon flies, lacewings and wasps.

Indiscriminate spraying is not recommended, as you can kill many helpful creatures at the same time as eliminating one or two types causing a particular problem.

Further information on pests and diseases can be found in the publication *Pests, Diseases and Ailments of Australian Plants* by Jones and Elliot, as listed in the Further Reading Section.

Plant diseases

The main diseases associated with the cultivation of Australian plants are fungal diseases.

Sooty mould is a black fungus which develops on stems and branches in association with the leaf-sucking scale insects. It can be removed by wiping stems with cool water to which a small amount of detergent has been added, and will generally be eliminated once the scale insects are removed.

Mildews, leaf spots and moulds are fungal diseases which often occur when there is insufficient air movement around plants. They can be particularly damaging on plants in glasshouses or other enclosed areas, where they can spread quickly. Any affected material should be removed as soon as it is noticed. Fungicidal sprays are available for the treatment of such diseases.

Ink disease is a problem caused by the combination of different fungi, which results in blackening of the leaves on kangaroo paws (*Anigozanthos* species). Some species are more susceptible than others, and healthy plants which are growing vigorously are also less likely to be affected than those which are languishing. Specific fungicides can be used as a means of control if necessary. Removal and burning of affected leaves is usually beneficial.

Collar-rot can occur at ground level, and is encouraged by organic mulch which is placed right up against the main stem or trunk. Poor drainage can also result in the occurrence of collar-rot. Eliminating the causes of collar-rot is the easiest method of control. After removing all damaged plant tissue with a sharp, clean implement, a fungicide such as bordeaux mixture can be used to assist the initial recovery of affected plants.

Root fungus can be a major problem, and cinnamon fungus, *Phytophthora cinnamomi* (also known as dieback), is a species of particular concern. It can affect many different types of ornamental plants, as well as some of the major food species. It is a water-borne fungus found in several natural areas of the world. Plants known to tolerate poor drainage are often resistant to it, but others from drier regions can be mildly to very susceptible.

Phytophthora cinnamomi is a disease which attacks the small feeder roots of plants, and cannot be accurately diagnosed without the use of a microscope. It is extremely difficult to eradicate, and efforts should therefore be made to avoid introducing it into a garden in the first place. Soil, sand, leaf litter or any other material should never be brought into a garden from bushland or other garden areas where a number of plants have died for no apparent reason. If you are walking or travelling by other means through any areas which you know or suspect may be affected by phytophthora, wash your shoes or car tyres, using a disinfectant. Only purchase plants from nurseries which are grown in sterilised or pasteurised potting mixes.

Fungicides are available which can help in preventing the spread of cinnamon fungus, and these can be used as a garden drench in areas affected by the problem. Further information can be obtained from nurseries or Agricultural Departments in each state of Australia.

Suppliers

Seed

Harper Seed Co., P.O. Box 315, Cannington, WA, 6107
H. G. Kershaw, P.O. Box 84, Terrey Hills, NSW, 2084
Nindethana Seed Service, R.M.B., Woogenilup, WA, 6324
Vaughans Wildflower Seeds, P.O. Box 66, Greenwood, WA, 6024
Western Australian Wildflower Society, P.O. Box 64, Nedlands, WA, 6009

Plants

Queensland
Fairhill Plants and Botanic Gardens, Fairhill Rd., Yandina, 4561
Lakkari Native Plant Nursery, Redland Bay Rd., Capalaba, 4157
Utingu Native Plant Nursery, Sorbiston St., Wellers Hill, 4121
Yaruga North Qld, Native Plant Nursery, Kennedy Highway, Walkamin, 4872

New South Wales
Annangrove Grevilleas, Annangrove Rd., Annangrove, 2156
Cranebrook Native Nursery, R23 Cranebrook Rd., Cranebrook, 2750
Floralands, Parry's Nurseries Pty. Ltd., Kariong via Gosford, 2250
Limpinwood Gardens, Limpinwood Valley via Chillingham, 2484
Sydney Wildflower Nursery, Namba Rd., Duffys Forest, 2084
Wirreanda Nursery, Wirreanda Rd., Ingleside, 2101

Australian Capital Territory
Rodney's Nursery, Pialligo Rd., Pialligo, 2609
Willow Park Nursery, Pialligo Rd., Pialligo, 2609

Victoria
Austraflora, Belfast Rd., Montrose, 3765
Austplant, Purves Rd., Main Ridge, Arthur's Seat, 3928
Bushwalk Native Plant Nursery, 58 Cranbourne Rd., Cranbourne Sth, 3977
Dragonfly Aquatics, RMB AB 366, Colac, 3250
Grevillea Nursery, 63 Railway Av., Werribee, 3030
Indigenous Plant Nurseries — c/- Secretary, Indigenous Flora & Fauna Association, 2/81 Alexandra Av., South Yarra, 3141
Kuranga Native Nursery, 393 Maroondah Highway, Ringwood, 3134
Treeplanters Nursery, Springvale Rd., Springvale South, 3172
Vicflora Nurseries, Alexandra, Benalla, Creswick, Dromana, Macedon, Mildura, Morwell River, Rennick and Wail
Westernport Nursery, 88 Flinders Rd., Bittern, 3918
White Gums Nursery, Glenorchy/Warracknabeal Rd., Stawell, 3380

Tasmania
Banksia Nurseries Pty. Ltd., Waratah Highway, Elliot, 7325
Murdunna Native Plant Nursery, Arthur Highway, Murdunna, 7172
Westland Nurseries at Kingston, Legana, Lenah Valley, Rocherlea and Sandy Bay
Woodbank Nursery, Huon Highway, Longley, 7150

South Australia
Benara Road Nursery, Benara Rd., Mt. Gambier, 5290
Nangula Native Plant Nursery, Nangula Springs via Millicent, 5280
Nellie Nursery, 46 Randell St., Mannum, 5238
Woods & Forests Department Nursery, Bremer Rd., Murray Bridge, 5253 also at Belair, Berri, Bundaleer, Cavan and Jamestown

Western Australia
Lullfitz Nursery, Cr. Capon & Honey Streets, Wanneroo, 6164
Wildflower Nurseries, 274 Wanneroo Rd., Lansdale, also at Kelmscott and Melville
Zanthorrea Nursery, 155 Watsonia Rd., Maida Vale, 6057

Northern Territory
Alice Springs Garden Nursery, Aranda Terrace, Alice Springs, 0870
Ironstone Lagoon Nursery, Lagoon Rd., Berrimah, 0828

These lists are not exhaustive but purely included as a guide to where seed and plants may be purchased. For further information on suppliers contact the Society for Growing Australian Plants in your state.

Further reading

Groundcovers, shrubs and trees

Australian Plant Study Group, (1980–85), *Grow What* Series, Thomas Nelson (Australia) Ltd., Melbourne

Elliot, G. M., (1985), *The Gardener's Guide to Australian Plants*, Hyland House, Melbourne

Elliot, G. M., (1988), *The New Australian Plants for Small Gardens and Containers*, Hyland House, Melbourne

Elliot, W. R. & Jones, D. L., *Encyclopaedia of Australian Plants Suitable for Cultivation*, Lothian Publishing Co., Melbourne

Food & Agriculture Organization, United Nations, (1979), *Eucalypts for Planting*, F.A.O. Rome, Italy

Harris, T. Y., (1977–80), *Gardening With Australian Plants* Series, Thomas Nelson (Australia) Ltd., Melbourne

Jones, D. L. & Gray, B. (1988), *Climbing Plants in Australia*, Reed Books Pty. Ltd., Frenchs Forest, NSW

Lord, E. E. and Willis, J. H., (1982), *Shrubs and Trees for Australian Gardens*, 5th Edition, Lothian Publishing Co., Melbourne

Simpfendorfer, K. J., (1975), *An Introduction to Trees for South Eastern Australia*, Inkata Press, Melbourne

Wrigley, J. W. & Fagg, M., (1988), *Australian Native Plants*, 3rd Edition, William Collins, Sydney

Orchids

Australasian Native Orchid Society (Vic. Group), *Cultivation of Australian Native Orchids*, A.N.O.S.

Jones, D. L., (1988), *Native Orchids of Australia*, Reed Books Pty. Ltd., Frenchs Forest, NSW

Ferns

Jones, D. L., (1987), *Encyclopaedia of Ferns*, Lothian Publishing Co., Melbourne

Jones, D. L. & Clemesha, S. C., (1976), *Australian Ferns and Fern Allies*, A. H. & A. W. Reed, Sydney

Australian plant propagation

Elliot, W. R. & Jones, D. L., (1989), *Encyclopaedia of Australian Plants Suitable for Cultivation*, Volume 1, Lothian Publishing Co., Melbourne

Gardiner, A., (1988), *Modern Plant Propagation*, Lothian Publishing Co., Melbourne

Garden design

Adams, G. M., (1980), *Birdscaping Your Garden*, Rigby, Adelaide

Lochhead, H., (1987), *Gardens for Living*, Greenhouse Publications, Richmond, Vic.

Molyneux, B. & Macdonald, R., (1983), *Native Gardens*, Thomas Nelson, Vic.

Niran, R., (1987), *Landscaping Your Garden*, Thomas Nelson, Vic.

Price, S. J., (1986), *The Urban Woodland*, Lothian Publishing Co., Melbourne

Readers Digest, (1973), *Practical Guide to Home Landscaping*, Readers Digest, Surry Hills, NSW

Stones, E., (1971), *Australian Garden Design*, Macmillan, Australia

Wilson, G., (1975), *Landscaping with Australian Plants*, Thomas Nelson, Vic.

Garden maintenance

Bradley, J., (1988), *Bringing Back the Bush*, Lansdowne, Sydney

C.S.I.R.O., *Discovering Soils Series*, C.S.I.R.O. Division of Soils, Melbourne

Elliot, R., (1984), *Pruning, a Practical Guide*, Lothian Publishing Co., Melbourne

Hockings, F. D., (1980), *Friends and Foes of Australian Gardens*, A. H. & A. W. Reed, Sydney

Jones, D. L. & Elliot, W. R., (1986), *Pests, Diseases & Ailments of Australian Plants*, Lothian Publishing Co., Melbourne

Lamp, C. & Collet, F., (1989), *A Field Guide to Weeds in Australia*, Inkata Press, Melbourne

Index